CW01371191

confidence.

8 STEPS TO KNOWING YOUR WORTH

Also by the Author

Manifest: 7 Steps to Living Your Best Life
Manifest: Dive Deeper
Manifest for Kids: Four Steps to Being the Best You

confidence.

8 STEPS TO KNOWING YOUR WORTH

ROXIE NAFOUSI

yellow kite

First published in Great Britain in 2025 by Yellow Kite
An imprint of Hodder & Stoughton Limited
An Hachette UK company

The authorised representative in the EEA is Hachette Ireland,
8 Castlecourt Centre, Dublin 15, D15 XTP3, Ireland (email: info@hbgi.ie)

1

Copyright © Roxie Nafousi 2025

The right of Roxie Nafousi to be identified as the Author of the
Work has been asserted by her in accordance with the Copyright,
Designs and Patents Act 1988.

This Work was edited by Arielle Steele.
Cover design by Amy Boyes.

All rights reserved. No part of this publication may be reproduced, stored in a
retrieval system, or transmitted, in any form or by any means without the prior
written permission of the publisher, nor be otherwise circulated in any form of
binding or cover other than that in which it is published and without a similar
condition being imposed on the subsequent purchaser.

A CIP catalogue record for this title is available from the British Library

Hardback ISBN 9781399734837
Trade Paperback ISBN 9781399734844
ebook ISBN 9781399734851

Typeset in Garamond MT Pro 10/12.5pt by Jouve (UK), Milton Keynes

Printed and bound in Great Britain by Clays Ltd, Elcograf S.p.A.

Hodder & Stoughton policy is to use papers that are natural, renewable
and recyclable products and made from wood grown in sustainable forests.
The logging and manufacturing processes are expected to conform to
the environmental regulations of the country of origin.

Hodder & Stoughton Limited
Carmelite House
50 Victoria Embankment
London EC4Y 0DZ

www.yellowkitebooks.co.uk

To my Dad,

Thank you for your wisdom, your selflessness,
your dedication and your love. You taught me the value
of hard work and perseverance, and the importance of a
positive mindset. You shaped me into the person
I am today and I am forever grateful to you.

I miss you and love you so much, x

CONTENTS

INTRODUCTION	1
My confidence journey	4
Why we need confidence	8
Why we struggle with confidence	11
Moving forward	14
STEP 1: Master Your Thoughts	17
STEP 2: Act with Intention	47
STEP 3: Stop Trying to Be Liked by Everybody	71
STEP 4: Break Free from Comparison	101
STEP 5: Celebrate Yourself	121
STEP 6: Do Hard Things	159
STEP 7: Be of Service to Others	181
STEP 8: Show Up as Your Best Self	201
EPILOGUE	227
GLOSSARY	231
ACKNOWLEDGEMENTS	233
SOURCES	235

INTRODUCTION

Confidence is the foundation of everything we do. It's the invisible force that shapes our choices, guides our actions and ultimately determines how we live our lives. It's what allows us to dream big, take risks and create a life we truly love. But for many of us, confidence can feel elusive – something reserved for those other people who seem to have it all figured out. This book is here to show you that confidence isn't an unattainable quality; it's something you can cultivate, nurture and grow.

Confidence can be defined in lots of different ways. Some say that it's about having belief in your abilities, judgements and qualities. Others define it as a person's trust in their capacity to handle tasks and challenges effectively. Some view confidence as a feeling of security and faith in oneself.

To me, confidence encompasses all of those things – and so much more. The way I see it, **true confidence is rooted in an unshakeable sense of self-worth**. It's about appreciating your inherent value. It's about accepting and valuing who you are, and all that you are. It's about trusting and respecting yourself and embracing all of your strengths and imperfections. Confidence means believing, without a shadow of a doubt, that you are deserving of all the love, success and abundance that life has to offer.

CONFIDENCE DOESN'T SHOUT.

Confidence can often be misunderstood. Many think it means being the loudest voice in the room, or that it's tied to a sense of superiority. But true confidence has nothing to do with being boastful or loud – it's not about standing above others. Instead, it's a state of being, **a way of moving through the world with purpose and assurance**. It's the voice inside you that says, 'I am worthy. I am enough.' It's the calm, unwavering belief that, whatever comes your way, *you can handle it*.

If you're reading this book, I know you've felt what it's like to lack confidence, and you're probably acutely aware of the countless ways in which it holds you back. You've felt the hesitation that stops you from speaking up, even when you know you have something valuable to say. You've experienced the fear that keeps you from pursuing opportunities, the doubt that makes you question your abilities and the feeling of being invisible when you so desperately want to be seen. You've felt the sting of comparing yourself to others and believing you fall short, the exhaustion of second-guessing every decision and the frustration of wanting more but feeling paralysed by your own insecurities.

Low self-esteem doesn't just sit quietly in the background – it infiltrates every aspect of your life. It affects your relationships, your career, your ambitions and the way you see yourself. It makes you shrink back when you should be stepping forward, and settling for less when you deserve so much more. It holds you back from everything you want, creating a gap between who you are and who you could be. And that's why you're here – because you're ready to close that gap and step into the confident, powerful version of yourself that you know, deep down, you're capable of becoming.

LACKING CONFIDENCE IS NOT A PERSONAL STRUGGLE; IT IS A GLOBAL ONE.

The confidence decline often starts young. Around 70 per cent of adolescents report feeling inadequate or lacking confidence. These are critical years for shaping self-identity, yet so many young people are struggling, carrying these insecurities into adulthood where they manifest as anxiety, depression and missed opportunities.

Research suggests that several mental health conditions, including depression, eating disorders and anxiety, are linked to low self-esteem.[1] And in today's digital world, social media only compounds this. According to a study from Pew Research Center, 23 per cent of teens said that what they see on social media makes them feel worse about their own lives.[2]

The workplace is not immune to the effects of low confidence either. We've all heard of imposter syndrome, something that makes talented individuals feel like frauds, constantly doubting their abilities and fearing that their success is undeserved. It's a pervasive issue that keeps people from stepping into leadership roles, sharing their ideas and striving to reach their goals. A KPMG study found that 75 per cent of women have experienced imposter syndrome in their careers.[3]

A survey by Dove also found that a staggering 85 per cent of women and 79 per cent of girls have opted out of important activities due to concerns about their appearance.[4] Lack of confidence isn't just holding individuals back – it's preventing millions of people from fully participating in their own lives, missing out on opportunities and experiences that could bring them joy and fulfilment.

It sounds bleak, I know. But here's the good news: **confidence can be cultivated and I am on a personal mission to help people to do just that.** Confidence is not a fixed trait – it's something that *can* be built and grown, step by step. And that's exactly why I wrote this book. *Confidence: 8 Steps to Knowing Your Worth* is more than just a guide – it's an invitation to unlock your full potential. It's about realising that you are already enough and that your worth isn't something you need to earn or prove.

CONFIDENCE IS NOT A LUXURY – IT'S THE KEY TO LIVING A FULFILLED, AUTHENTIC LIFE. WITHOUT IT, WE'RE HELD HOSTAGE BY OUR OWN INSECURITIES.

MY CONFIDENCE JOURNEY

As an Iraqi girl growing up in Oxford, England, I was acutely aware that I didn't fit in. I noticed my differences early on: my olive skin, dark curly hair and the distinct cultural traditions we observed at home, from the food we ate to the holidays we celebrated. At primary school, these differences set me apart: the other kids often left me out at playtime or didn't pick me for their teams, and, from there, my self-rejection began. I became ashamed of my culture and who I was. This only got worse after the tragic events of 9/11, when the world was filled with misconceptions and judgements about my heritage. I no longer felt I belonged anywhere – I was rejecting my culture at home, while simultaneously feeling rejected by the rest of the world.

But it wasn't just where I was from, I also despised the way I looked. I distinctly remember the first time I felt ugly. I was seven years old, looking in the mirror in the downstairs bathroom, fixating on the dark circles under my too-big eyes, droopy eyebrows and crooked teeth. This fixation grew with me, and I spent most of my life obsessed with the fact that I was 'hideous' and 'a monster'. I was certain that my ugliness was the reason that boys rejected me, why I wasn't one of the 'popular girls' and why I was so often ridiculed by my peers.

When I was 11, my 'best friend' told me that everyone was talking about how pointy my chin was – only adding to my ever-growing list of insecurities. At 12, a boy in my class told me 'You'd be hotter if you fixed your teeth and sorted out your acne.' And then aged 14, a girl in the year above me at school commented on my Bebo page that I looked like I'd eaten more than enough cupcakes – *enter disordered eating*. I wore coloured contact lenses for six years (masking my dark brown eyes with bright blue lenses), straightened my hair every day, applied way too much make-up and then even went so far as to have a rhinoplasty (nose job) in my late twenties. But, no matter what I did on the outside, the intense self-hatred and constant dialogue of my inner critic never stopped.

When I think back, I feel sad about how much time, energy and life I lost and missed out on. There was so much that I didn't do just because I never felt good enough. The insecurities, doubts and limiting beliefs left me stuck in a cycle of unhappiness. Looking back, it's no wonder that when I first drank alcohol and took drugs, I found the false sense of confidence they gave me so addictive. It was an escape from the self-hate – a way to feel, even for a short while, that I was someone I liked, someone who belonged.

But, of course, those substances were only temporary solutions. They masked the pain without ever healing it. As I got older, the reality of my life started to clash with the hopes I once had for myself. I wanted to be happy, successful, loved and at peace, but I could never get there as long as I carried so much shame and self-loathing. I reached a breaking point in May 2018, when I hit rock bottom and realised I couldn't keep living this way. Around that time, I came across a podcast about something called 'manifestation'. The hosts talked about how manifesting was rooted in self-worth – the idea that we create a life that reflects what we believe we deserve. And I thought, *If I have no self-worth, then no wonder I'm keeping myself stuck.*

This was the beginning of my transformation. I started to learn more about manifestation, not just as a tool to achieve goals or attract things into my orbit, but as a profound shift in how I saw myself, how I felt about myself and how I showed up for myself. I realised that the biggest obstacle in my life wasn't my past, my culture or the way I looked – it was the beliefs I held about my worth.

One of the first steps I took was to embrace my differences rather than reject them. I let go of the things I used to hide about myself – ditching the coloured contacts and beginning to reconnect with my roots. While these were survival tactics when I was younger, as an adult, I had to learn to love both versions of myself. I started to embrace my cultural heritage and the unique identity that made me who I was. I also began to heal my relationship with my body, recognising that no amount of external change could fix how I felt about myself internally. I had to do the inner work to truly recognise my worth.

Manifestation and confidence are deeply intertwined. The greatest gift that manifesting gave me was the ability to help me step into my power and realise my potential. The more I worked on my confidence, the more powerfully I was able to manifest the life I desired. In 2021 and 2022, I used my experiences and learnings to guide me as I wrote my debut books *MANIFEST* and *MANIFEST: Dive Deeper*, books that went on to reach over one million people globally. Writing them wasn't just about teaching manifestation techniques; it was also about sharing how transforming our mindsets – and ultimately our confidence – can change our lives in the most magical and incredible ways.

That's what I want you to understand as you read this book: confidence isn't just an add-on to your manifesting journey; it's at the core of it. The more confident we are, the more we believe in our potential and the more powerfully we can create the lives we deserve to be living. That said, this book is a journey you can take on its own – whether or not you're familiar with manifestation.

THIS BOOK IS A GUIDE TO HELP YOU BUILD AND CULTIVATE CONFIDENCE FROM WITHIN, IN EVERY ASPECT OF YOUR LIFE.

Confidence has completely transformed my life. It's the foundation that allows me to show up as myself, to embrace opportunities and to trust in my ability to handle whatever comes my way. But the confidence I have now didn't come to me in a single breakthrough moment. It was a gradual process, one where I had to make a commitment to honour myself, to be kind to myself and to act like the person I wanted to become. And my confidence journey is still ongoing. Every day, I make the choice to step into my worth and live as my most authentic self. I've learned that confidence isn't about being perfect or never feeling fear – it's about trusting yourself enough to take action despite those things. It's about allowing yourself to be vulnerable, to make mistakes and to always be willing to learn.

I share my journey because I want you to see that confidence is something we can all develop, no matter where you start or how broken you may feel. You have the power to redefine who you are, silence your inner critic and embody the person you were always meant to be. Confidence isn't about fitting in or being accepted by others – it's about fully accepting yourself and allowing your true light to shine.

I want you to know that you are not alone in this pursuit. We all have our struggles, our insecurities and our fears. But the very things you believe make you unworthy are actually what make you beautifully and uniquely you. This book is my invitation to you to help you step into your power, to build a confidence that comes from within and to change your life. The path may not always be easy, but I promise you, it's worth it. And you're not walking it alone – I am here with you every step of the way. **You are enough, just as you are, and you deserve to live a life filled with love, joy and unshakeable confidence.**

WHY WE NEED CONFIDENCE

In psychology, confidence is seen as an essential stepping stone for living a fulfilled life. In 1954, a psychologist called Abraham Maslow developed 'Maslow's Hierarchy of Needs', which categorises human needs into five levels, ranging from the most basic needs to more complex psychological and self-fulfilment needs.[5] Here's what it looks like:

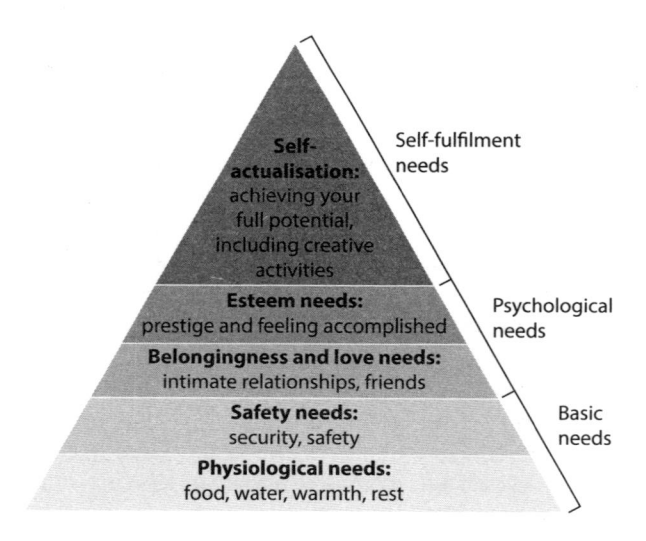

Self-actualisation: achieving your full potential, including creative activities — Self-fulfilment needs

Esteem needs: prestige and feeling accomplished
Belongingness and love needs: intimate relationships, friends — Psychological needs

Safety needs: security, safety
Physiological needs: food, water, warmth, rest — Basic needs

The model suggests that, once humans have all our basic needs met — food, water, warmth, rest, shelter and safety — it then becomes more possible to meet our psychological needs. According to Maslow, one of these essential needs is self-esteem: the feeling that we are competent, capable and worthy.

When we have good self-esteem (and therefore confidence), we're in a much better position to ascend to the peak of the pyramid, **self-actualisation**, which you could also describe as fulfilment. This is where we explore our talents, take on challenges and strive for personal growth. It's also where we begin to seek purpose and look beyond ourselves. Confidence is what allows us to engage with the world, build meaningful relationships, pursue our goals and discover who we are meant to be. Simply put, **confidence isn't just a 'nice-to-have' – it's an essential part of the human experience**. We all need it, we all deserve it and, most importantly, we can all achieve it.

Research has found that confidence positively impacts almost every area of our lives. Here are a few examples:

1. **We excel in the workplace:** Research shows that having confidence can be a key driver of both workplace satisfaction and financial success.[6] A study on workplace behaviours found that people with higher self-esteem were more likely to take initiative, negotiate well and collaborate effectively.[7] The study also found that those who were more confident felt more satisfied at work.
2. **It can protect against anxiety, depression and stress:** In one study, researchers assessed adolescents with pre-existing psychiatric problems over a three-year period.[8] They found that participants who had higher self-esteem as their baseline predicted fewer symptoms of anxiety, depression and attention problems three years later. Another study on young people also found that self-esteem improved resilience to stress.[9]
3. **It helps us attract potential partners:** You'll probably already know that confidence is the most attractive quality in a potential partner, and studies have backed this up. Research has discovered that individuals who perceive themselves as confident

are often rated as more attractive by others. Confidence has also been shown to increase desirability in dating scenarios, with confident people being perceived as more socially and romantically appealing.[10]

4. **We thrive in social situations:** Research suggests that people with high self-esteem tend to have better social relationships.[11] That's because confidence helps us to approach new people, and develop meaningful connections with people we already know.

5. **We build successful romantic relationships:** Research has shown that confidence helps to create healthier relationship dynamics.[12] This happens for a few different reasons: it allows us to express our needs, desires and boundaries, and resolve conflicts effectively. It's also beneficial for fostering secure attachment, trust and emotional security; when we're more secure in ourselves, we're less likely to lean on our partners for validation; *and* the more confident we feel, the less likely we are to project our insecurities and anxieties into our romantic relationships.

6. **We become more creative:** When we are restricted by limiting beliefs, we place boundaries on what we believe is possible. But when we are confident, we're more likely to take risks, innovate and think outside the box. One study found that people who were confident in their creative abilities tended to produce more original ideas.[13] Research has also shown that when we are confident, we rely less on approval from other people, which creates more possibilities for authentic self-expression.[14]

WHY WE STRUGGLE WITH CONFIDENCE

Now that we understand that confidence is a shared struggle for so many of us, and why we need it, let's explore *why* so many of us grapple with it.

I believe there are four main reasons why confidence issues are so widespread – though these reasons are deeply interlinked. These themes will come up repeatedly throughout the eight steps, but I want to outline them here briefly to help you start reflecting on where your own self-doubt might stem from.

Our brains

The human mind is hardwired to focus on the negative more than the positive – what psychologists call the **negativity bias**. This evolutionary trait made sense for our ancestors, who needed to be hyper-aware of danger to survive threats like predators. Negative experiences often indicated immediate danger, so our brains evolved to prioritise them.

Today, however, we aren't facing life-threatening predators – we're dealing with a difficult boss, snarky comments or the pressures of social media. The problem is, our brains often struggle to differentiate between genuine threats and everyday stressors. This leads us to overreact to criticism or negative feedback as if our survival is at stake.

As a result, we are more likely to remember and internalise setbacks than celebrate our achievements. The negativity bias that once protected us now traps us in cycles of self-doubt, amplifying fears and insecurities. In Step 1: Master Your Thoughts we'll explore how our minds can work against us – and, more importantly, how we can change that.

Parenting and childhood

Our upbringing plays a profound role in shaping how we see ourselves as adults. Even if your childhood wasn't what you'd describe as 'traumatic', certain experiences can still leave lasting marks on your confidence.

Dr Gabor Maté, renowned for his work on trauma, has helped expand the definition of trauma to include not only overtly traumatic events but also seemingly minor moments that impact our sense of self-worth.[15] He describes trauma not as the event itself, but as the way the event impacts a person's psyche. Perhaps you were often criticised for being 'too loud' or 'messy', which may have led you to believe that certain parts of yourself were unacceptable.

Even positive reinforcement can have unintended effects. If you were constantly praised for being 'clever' or 'pretty', you may have learned to tie your value solely to those qualities, creating a fragile sense of worth that depends on external validation.

It's not about blaming our parents/caregivers – they were doing the best they could, often based on their own upbringing. But it's important to acknowledge how these early experiences can deeply influence our confidence and shape the narrative we carry about ourselves into adulthood.

Peer groups and friendships

The need for belonging is a fundamental part of being human. As we just explored, according to Maslow's Hierarchy of Needs, feeling loved and accepted is one of our core psychological needs. Our survival once depended on being part of a group – our 'tribe' – which is why the instinct to fit in is so deeply ingrained. It's not surprising, then, that our peer groups have a significant impact on our confidence.

This need for belonging starts young. I became aware of this last year with my then four-year-old son, Wolfe. He had just started school and, as the temperature dropped, he needed a hat. So, I went to the shops and bought him a Spider-Man hat, as he loved Spider-Man at the time. But every time I tried to get him to wear it, he refused. Eventually, he explained why. He said, 'Mummy, I'm scared the other boys will laugh at me.' It broke my heart. Even at such a young age, he was aware of the need to fit in.

As children, we become acutely conscious of our differences, and school becomes a breeding ground for comparison. Experiences of teasing, feeling left out or struggling to fit in can leave lasting scars. As we grow, the desire to belong never really leaves us, and the fear of rejection or exclusion often undercuts our ability to feel fully confident. In Step 3: Stop Trying to Be Liked by Everybody we will work to undo some of this damage.

Society and culture

Society has always dictated what is 'worthy', desirable and beautiful, and these ideals are constantly shifting. Growing up in the 1990s, I idolised the slim, blonde, blue-eyed women who were glorified in magazines and on TV. I measured myself against them and, when I didn't match up, I felt inadequate. Every piece of culture we consume – whether it's advertisements, movies, books or music – contributes to our perception of what is desirable and what is not.

Even though today's culture is making strides towards greater diversity, social media has amplified the pressure to compare ourselves to others. We are bombarded with curated, filtered images of perfection that highlight our perceived flaws. Constant exposure to these idealised lives can make us feel as though we're falling short, feeding into feelings of inadequacy and undermining our self-worth. In Step 4: Break Free from Comparison, we'll delve deeper into how social media and modern culture impact our confidence and how we can navigate this overwhelming landscape.

MOVING FORWARD

With all of this in mind, it's crucial to remember not to be so hard on yourself. Given all the pressures – from our upbringing, our social environments and the unrealistic ideals set by society – it's no wonder that many of us struggle with confidence. But there's hope. Even when the odds feel stacked against you, it's absolutely possible to overcome these challenges and transform into your most confident self, and I am here to show you how.

WELCOME TO YOUR CONFIDENCE JOURNEY.

In this book, I want to help you overcome the barriers that are damaging your self-worth and ultimately preventing you from living life to the fullest. Through eight steps, we'll explore how to build genuine confidence from the inside out. Not the kind that's about putting on a brave face or pretending you've got it all together, but the kind that's rooted in self-acceptance, resilience and a deep understanding of your own value.

My eight steps for building confidence are:

- Step 1: Master Your Thoughts
- Step 2: Act with Intention
- Step 3: Stop Trying to Be Liked by Everybody
- Step 4: Break Free from Comparison
- Step 5: Celebrate Yourself
- Step 6: Do Hard Things
- Step 7: Be of Service to Others
- Step 8: Show Up as Your Best Self

Within each step, you'll find the tools that I've both used myself and shared with my clients and in workshops – tried-and-tested methods for building your confidence. I recommend working through this book in order, as the earlier steps lay the foundation for the later ones. However, once you've read through it once, I encourage you to come back again, jump around the chapters and try using different tools whenever they resonate.

There are several different terms that orbit around the word 'confidence' and I've included a Glossary on page 231 explaining these. You'll notice that these terms will come up frequently as you work through the steps.

I can't wait for you to meet the most confident version of yourself. Let's begin . . .

> **Note:** This book is designed to help you cultivate confidence, transform your mindset and take powerful steps towards creating the life you deserve. However, if you are struggling with serious mental health challenges, I encourage you to seek professional help alongside this journey. Therapy, counselling or other forms of professional support can provide the care and guidance you need to heal and grow. Remember, seeking help is a sign of strength, and combining it with the tools in this book can be a powerful step towards lasting change.

STEP 1

MASTER YOUR THOUGHTS

*Our thoughts shape our beliefs,
and our beliefs shape our reality.*

ROXIE NAFOUSI — CONFIDENCE

Everything begins with a thought.

Our thoughts influence the way we feel, drive our behaviour and ultimately form the foundation of our self-worth. Mastering your thoughts is not just about positive thinking – it's about reclaiming control over your mind, silencing the self-doubt and rewriting the negative narratives that have held you back for far too long.

If we repeat a thought often enough, it transforms into a belief. For example, if you struggled making friends at school, you might have had recurring thoughts like, 'People don't like me,' or 'I'm not good at making friends.' Over time, these thoughts solidify into beliefs and you begin to internalise the idea that you're not sociable or likeable. Once this belief takes hold, **it becomes the filter through which you interpret the world**, impacting your decisions, perceptions and behaviours.

Marisa Peer, the world-renowned therapist, says, 'Your mind's job is to make your thoughts real.'[1] In other words, our minds will always try to find evidence to support the beliefs we hold, whether they are empowering or limiting. Imagine you're at a party, and you believe that people don't like you. Because of this belief, you may enter feeling self-conscious, avoid eye contact, hesitate to start conversations or stand alone. And any neutral response from others might be misinterpreted as rejection, reinforcing your belief that you're unlikeable and creating a cycle that keeps you feeling isolated.

Most of the time, we don't consciously notice the thoughts that pass through our minds or realise the extent to which they shape our reality. And the more deeply embedded these beliefs become, the harder it feels to challenge them. You may start to believe that 'this is just who I am' rather than recognising these beliefs as patterns that were learned – and, more importantly, that can be unlearned.

Our beliefs determine how we perceive situations, how we interpret events and, ultimately, how we define ourselves. They become self-fulfilling prophecies, for better or for worse.

Let me give you another example. Imagine you're about to interview for your dream job, but you believe, 'I am not deserving of this opportunity.' This belief will put you at a disadvantage before you even begin. It affects how you feel, which can lead you to downplay your skills, hesitate to express your enthusiasm or avoid highlighting your accomplishments. The interviewer may notice your reluctance and interpret it as a lack of interest or capability, which will ultimately affect their perception of you. Your belief, though untrue, becomes a self-fulfilling prophecy.

Research backs this up; a study found that confidence in an interview directly impacts the likelihood of securing a job.[2] When you lack confidence, it reflects in your body language, your tone and your responses. If you don't get the job, it reinforces your negative beliefs, and the cycle continues into the next opportunity and the one after that.

Our limiting beliefs keep us trapped, but the good news is that you have the power to break free. By mastering your thoughts, you can challenge the beliefs that are holding you back and replace them with ones that will empower you to unlock your fullest potential.

THE INNER CRITIC

'If people get to know you, you do know they'll leave you, don't you? Everyone thinks you are such a loser. You'll never be good enough. Everyone else is better than you, why can't you be more like them?'

This was pretty much the running commentary I lived with for most of my life. No, they weren't the cruel words of an emotionally abusive partner or a bully at school. Instead, they came from the voice in my own mind. Sadly, I know many of you reading this can relate.

Your inner critic is one of the biggest barriers to confidence. It is the relentless voice that pokes at your insecurities to remind you of what you're lacking and all the things you are not. It is the voice that points out your flaws and magnifies your doubts until you feel inadequate and unworthy. Our inner critic is the voice that slowly but surely chips away at our confidence and gives power to our limiting beliefs.

Before we can begin to overpower the inner critic, we must first become aware of it. **Self-awareness is the first step of any personal change.** In the exercise opposite, I've created space for you to identify your inner critic, the things it says *and* when and in what circumstances its voice becomes the loudest.

✏️ EXERCISE: INNER CRITIC AWARENESS

Set aside 10–15 minutes in a quiet space where you won't be disturbed. Grab a journal or notebook and take some time to reflect on your day or week, writing down any negative thoughts or statements you remember saying to yourself.

As you do this, know that it's normal to feel emotional. Feeling sadness or compassion while doing this exercise means you're recognising the harshness you've endured from your own mind, and that's an important part of the healing process. *Why?* Because only when you allow yourself to fully feel and acknowledge the pain caused by your inner critic can you begin to release it.

Be as specific as you can, and use the questions below to guide your reflection.

- What are the common negative statements you say to yourself?
- In what situations or experiences do these statements show up? For example, at work/in your relationships/ at the gym/when you look in the mirror.
- When your inner critic tells you these things, how does it make you feel? Be really specific. Do you feel ashamed? Anxious? Guilty? Sad? Worthless?

Well done for being vulnerable and identifying the inner critic. It's not always easy, but it's a powerful first step towards change.

Once you've identified the thoughts your inner critic tends to repeat, the next step is to try to understand where these thoughts come from. The critical voice we hear today almost always has its roots in past experiences and old wounds. To disempower your inner critic, we need to uncover these origins so that you can begin to change them.

When I work with private clients, the first thing I do is ask them to talk me through their entire life story, starting as far back as they can remember. I encourage them to share everything they feel comfortable with, reminding them that even seemingly insignificant memories are worth mentioning.

One of my clients, for instance, initially came to me because he struggled to show emotion in his new relationship. He felt closed off and unable to express his love, even though he knew he deeply cared for his partner. It was only after he had told me his life story that we could begin to explore where these behaviours came from. As he spoke about his past, he began to see the connections. He recalled that his mother left the family when he was 13, which made him associate love with abandonment. Later, when his first serious girlfriend broke up with him shortly after he said, 'I love you,' it reinforced the idea that expressing love led to rejection and pain. From that point, emotional barriers went up and stayed there, protecting him from potential heartbreak, but also keeping him emotionally distant.

On drawing the connections, he was able to do three things:

1. Feel compassion for himself and his behaviours because he finally understood their root cause.
2. Create space to view his current relationship more objectively, free from the influence of old wounds.
3. Identify where deeper healing was necessary to move forward.

We can do the same thing with our inner critic by connecting it to our past experiences. By recognising that your inner critic's voice stems from specific moments in your life, you can begin to see it for what it is: not an objective truth, but a story you've internalised.

Uncovering the roots of our limiting beliefs shines a light on how long they've been influencing our self-perception, shaping the way we think, behave and view the world around us.

▶ EXERCISE: REFLECT ON YOUR LIFE EXPERIENCES TO UNDERSTAND YOUR INNER CRITIC

This powerful exercise draws on the work I do with my clients, and focuses on delving into your past experiences to uncover *why* your inner critic says the things it does.

> **Note:** This kind of self-exploration can bring up uncomfortable or even traumatic memories. It's important to approach this exercise with compassion and care for yourself. If you find the process overwhelming, pause and take a step back. You don't have to confront everything all at once – progress only as and when you feel ready and safe to do so. If you feel that these reflections are too difficult to handle on your own, I encourage you to seek the support of a therapist or counsellor who can help guide you through this process.

Stage 1: Connect the belief
Reflect on the negative statements you noted earlier. What core beliefs do these statements represent? For instance, if your inner critic often says, 'My partner doesn't love me,' could this reflect a deeper belief that 'I am unloveable,' or 'I am not deserving of love'?

Stage 2: Find the root
Of the beliefs you've identified, can you recall experiences that may have planted these seeds of self-doubt? Reflect on both the first instance when this belief might have formed and any other subsequent moments that reinforced it.

Deep dive: Advanced reflection
If you feel ready to explore this concept further, consider this additional exercise to gain deeper insights into your inner critic:

- List the most significant life experiences you can remember, focusing on moments that stand out as pivotal or memorable. Aim for at least two key moments from each stage of your life (for example, early childhood, adolescence, early adulthood). These could be times when you felt judged, inadequate or not good enough.
- As you create your list, look for any patterns or connections to your current life and situations – what do these experiences have in common? Are there any 'aha' moments that help you understand the voice of your inner critic?

This exercise has actually become a natural part of my day-to-day life. Whenever I catch myself saying something negative, I pause and wonder where it's really coming from. Is it an old belief? A past experience? This habit of self-awareness helps me interrupt patterns, view things more objectively and approach myself with more kindness and understanding. Over time, this practice can become second nature, helping you to create a healthier, more supportive inner dialogue.

Recognising the inner critic and identifying its source is the first step to change. Once we have done this, we can start to find ways to rewrite our thoughts.

To do this, there are three principles I want you to be aware of:

You are not your thoughts
You might often feel overwhelmed by negative thoughts, but it's important to understand that you are not your thoughts – you are simply the observer of them. This means that just because a thought pops into your head, it doesn't mean that it defines you. When you recognise that you can watch your thoughts without letting them take over, it gives you the power to step back and choose how to respond.

When we achieve this separation, we can respond to situations more calmly, thoughtfully and effectively, rather than reacting impulsively based on fleeting or irrational thoughts.

Just because you think something, doesn't mean it's true
Thoughts are not necessarily reflections of reality; they are often subjective interpretations influenced by our emotions, biases, past experiences and cognitive distortions, which we will explore shortly.

Not every thought that arises should be believed or acted upon. It's crucial to develop the ability to discern between thoughts that are helpful and those that are harmful or simply untrue. This awareness can help us avoid falling into negative spirals of self-doubt.

You have more control than you realise
While we may not be able to stop negative and critical thoughts from arising, we *can* choose how to engage with them. This control comes from the ability to question, challenge and reframe our thoughts. We will explore effective ways to question our thoughts shortly.

FAQ:

Q: What's the difference between the subconscious and the conscious mind?

A: Your *conscious mind* is responsible for whatever you are actively thinking about at any given moment. It's the part of your mind that processes current thoughts and turns them into actions. It's deliberate, rational and where your immediate decisions are made.

Your *subconscious mind* is what lies beneath the surface. It draws on everything you have learned and stored in your brain. It holds all your memories, deep-rooted beliefs, automatic behaviours and emotional reactions. It's estimated that 95 per cent of our brain's activity happens in the subconscious mind, making it an incredibly powerful influence on our everyday lives.

THE POWER OF COGNITIVE BIASES

Our brains are constantly bombarded with an overwhelming amount of information – some scientists estimate that we process as much as 74GB of information daily, which is equivalent to watching 16 movies.[3] To cope with this enormous volume, our subconscious mind does a lot of heavy lifting behind the scenes, filtering and organising information so we can function effectively. One of the ways it does this is through **cognitive biases** – mental shortcuts that help us sort through what's important and what can be discarded.

Many of these shortcuts are helpful to us in day-to-day life. For instance, when you read a sentence, your brain doesn't process each word individually. Instead, it quickly recognises familiar words and phrases, allowing you to understand the sentence as a whole almost instantly. This ability to read and comprehend quickly is a result of your brain's ability to create shortcuts based on previous experience and knowledge, making the process more efficient and less mentally taxing.

Another example is when you walk into a crowded room. Your brain rapidly scans the faces around you. This quick identification is a mental shortcut that saves time and energy, allowing you to focus on more meaningful interactions rather than spending time figuring out who everyone is.

However, not all shortcuts are helpful. Some, like stereotyping, are harmful. Stereotyping is a way for the brain to simplify social interactions by placing people into categories based on limited information, which can lead to unfair judgements and even discrimination.

Cognitive biases are common mistakes in thinking that happen when our brains try to quickly make sense of information. These mental shortcuts help us process things faster, but they often lead to errors because they are influenced by our past experiences, beliefs and emotions.

One common bias is called the **frequency illusion**, which makes our brains notice things we focus on, making them seem more common than they actually are. This happens a lot in everyday life. For example, have you ever bought a new car and then suddenly it seems as though every other car on the road is the same? Or I remember when I cut a fringe into my hair, and the next time I was on social media, it suddenly seemed that everyone else had a fringe too. Obviously, this wasn't the case – my brain was simply tuning in to something that I was focused on, giving the illusion that it was suddenly more prevalent than it really was.

Another common bias is **confirmation bias**, where we tend to seek out information or interpret events in a way that confirms our pre-existing beliefs. For example, if you believe you're not good at public speaking, your brain will be on high alert for evidence that supports this belief. You might vividly remember the times you stumbled over your words but forget the moments when you spoke confidently and clearly.

But this bias doesn't always work against us – it can also be used to our advantage. Imagine you hold a belief that you are capable and deserving of success. When you walk into a meeting feeling prepared and confident, you are more likely to notice positive reactions, like a colleague nodding in agreement or someone giving you a compliment afterwards. Your brain picks up on these signals and uses them to reinforce your belief in yourself, creating a positive feedback loop. This not only boosts your confidence in the moment, but also improves your performance even more. The belief you hold becomes self-reinforcing, helping you show up at your best.

YOUR BRAIN IS PRIMED TO CONFIRM WHAT IT ALREADY BELIEVES TO BE TRUE, RATHER THAN NOTICING CUES THAT WOULD GIVE YOU AN ALTERNATIVE NARRATIVE.

Understanding cognitive biases is crucial because these biases can distort our perception of reality, often reinforcing negative self-perceptions and limiting beliefs. By recognising and acknowledging these biases, we can begin to challenge our thoughts, see situations more objectively and start building a more resilient, confident mindset. Throughout the steps in this book, we'll revisit cognitive biases and discuss how they come into play in different situations.

THOUGHT FILTERS
(COGNITIVE DISTORTIONS)

Our brains also save time and energy through the use of **cognitive distortions** or, as I like to call them, **'thought filters'**. While cognitive biases generally influence how we interpret the world around us, cognitive distortions are specific errors in thinking that often arise in our own internal dialogue.

To help illustrate the difference, think of cognitive biases as mental shortcuts that our brain uses to make sense of the world around us and make decisions. They can lead to distorted perceptions of the world. On the other hand, cognitive distortions are specific thinking errors that tend to reinforce negative beliefs, often related to self-esteem or mental health.

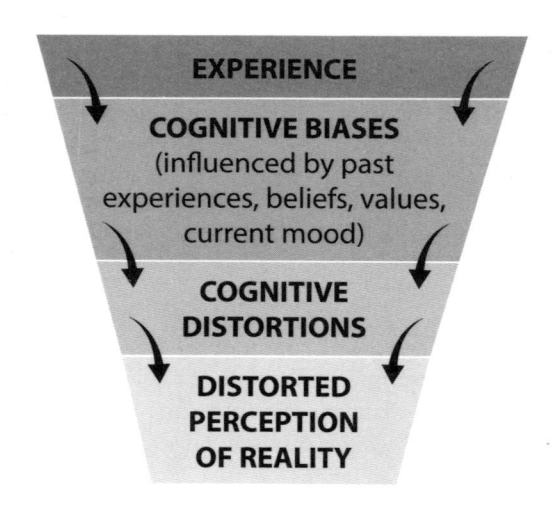

EXPERIENCE

COGNITIVE BIASES
(influenced by past experiences, beliefs, values, current mood)

COGNITIVE DISTORTIONS

DISTORTED PERCEPTION OF REALITY

The different thought filters
There are several types of thought filters we use, and each one can have a significant impact on our mental health and overall well-being. By understanding these thought filters, we can begin to see how they shape our view of ourselves and start working to challenge them.

All-or-nothing thinking
This thought filter causes us to see things in black-and-white terms – something is either all good or all bad, a total success or a complete failure. There's no middle ground.

Example: If you set a goal to exercise every day for a week and you miss a day, you may conclude that you've completely failed, ignoring the progress you made on the other days.

Catastrophising
This is when you expect the worst-case scenario to happen or you exaggerate the severity of a situation. It can create an intense fear of failure and amplifies stress and anxiety. You avoid facing (and therefore overcoming) challenges, which are necessary for building confidence and resilience, because your distorted assumption says, 'If I fail, the outcome will be catastrophic.'

Example: You have to send a presentation to a client but your mind spirals: you assume they will dislike what they see and then doubt your competency altogether. You imagine that they might escalate the issue and you lose your job over it.

Sieving
This type of thinking makes you ignore the positives and focus only on the negatives. For example, if you receive ten compliments and one criticism, the 'sieve' only catches the criticism, while the compliments are dismissed or ignored. This process reinforces negative self-perceptions.

Example: You look through the reviews on your company's website. The majority are filled with admiration and praise, but there is one with constructive feedback, and one less pleasant review. Instead of feeling proud of the kind ones, you fixate on the criticism, feeling like you're not good enough.

Personalising

I think this is one of the most common thought filters that we use, and it's one that I used to struggle with a lot. Personalising means blaming yourself for events that are outside of your control or interpreting negative external events as being directly related to you, even when there's no evidence to support that assumption.

Example:
- Your team loses a game, and you think, 'It's my fault we lost.'
- Someone doesn't reply to your message, and you assume it means they don't like you.
- A friend cancels plans, and you think, 'They must be tired of me,' even though they said they had a family emergency.

Over-generalising

This happens when you take an isolated negative event and assume that it will happen over and over again. Over-generalising can prevent you from persevering through challenges and ultimately from experiencing growth and progress.

Example: You go on a date that doesn't go well and, instead of seeing it as just one bad date, you think, 'I'm terrible at dating. I'll never find anyone.'

> **Note:** There are more filters, but these are the ones I felt were most relevant. For more information, search for 'cognitive distortions' on PositivePsychology.com.

Understanding and recognising the thought filters we use is crucial because they often create inaccurate and unkind versions of reality that negatively impact our self-esteem. Learning about them has personally helped me to understand that my thoughts are not objective, and they are not always based on reality. I began to view cognitive thought filters just like a TikTok filter: you still see a version of the picture, but it's not the real, original picture. It has been edited and warped, and the result is exaggerated at best, and completely different at worst.

▶ EXERCISE: OVERCOME COGNITIVE DISTORTIONS

Use the table opposite to track your thoughts, the filters you identify and what a more balanced, realistic version of those thoughts might be. I've included some examples to start you off.

Keep this practice ongoing, as repeated awareness is key to change.

Event	Filtered Thought	Thought Filter	Realistic Thought
I send a text to the group WhatsApp – and no one responds.	'Everyone finds me annoying.'	Personalising	'They're all busy people and sometimes messages get missed.'
My boss sends an email that reads: 'Do you have five minutes for a quick chat?'	'Oh no, I've clearly been doing a terrible job and they're going to sack me.'	Catastrophising	'There could be any number of reasons why my boss needs to speak to me.'

Interview your thoughts

Earlier, I shared three principles: you are not your thoughts; just because you think something doesn't mean it's true; and you have more control than you realise. Recognising 'thought filters' helps you see how distorted thinking can keep you stuck.

But awareness alone isn't enough – what you need is a practical way to challenge these thoughts and reshape them into ones that serve you better.

That's where 'interviewing your thoughts' comes in. Inspired by Socratic questioning, this approach helps you step back and evaluate your beliefs from different angles. Imagine yourself as a detective, determined to uncover the real story by examining the facts, challenging assumptions and considering different viewpoints.

Below, I've provided a set of questions to help you 'interview' your thoughts. I encourage you to take a picture of these questions and save it on your phone, so they're handy whenever negative thinking feels overwhelming. The more you practise, the more naturally these questions will come to you – helping you reach a more balanced and empowering perspective faster.

Present the evidence
- What evidence do I have that supports this thought?
- Is there any evidence that contradicts it?

Challenge assumptions
- What assumptions am I making here?
- Are those assumptions justified or am I jumping to conclusions?

Identify the cause
- Could past experiences be influencing my current thinking?
- Is it possible that I'm reacting based on an old fear or memory rather than what's happening right now?

Consider different perspectives
- How would I view this situation if I were an outsider?
- What advice would I give to a friend who felt this way?

Examine the consequences
- If I continue thinking like this, what's the likely outcome?
- How might this thought be holding me back from what I want?

Explore alternatives
- Is there another, more positive or realistic way to interpret this situation?
- What might be a more helpful or balanced way to think about this?

By systematically questioning your thoughts, you begin to strip away layers of negativity and reveal a clearer, more truthful perspective. Practising these questions will build your ability to catch and challenge negative thinking, replacing it with a mindset that supports your growth and confidence.

THE HECKLER VERSUS THE CHEERLEADER

Now that we've learned how to challenge and question our negative thoughts, it's time to take things a step further. It's not enough to simply silence the inner critic – we need to replace that negative voice with something more supportive and encouraging. This is where I want to introduce a powerful new concept that has helped me overpower my own inner critic: 'the heckler versus the cheerleader'.

Our inner dialogue has a huge impact on how we feel about ourselves and, in turn, how we show up in the world. The voice we allow to dominate can either propel us forward or keep us stuck.

Think of it like this: imagine you're a comedian on stage. If the audience is constantly heckling you, shouting that your jokes are terrible and booing you off the stage, it's going to be incredibly hard for you to perform at your best. Now, imagine that the audience is encouraging you with warm smiles and laughing at all your jokes when you hoped they would. You would feel so much more confident on stage, and your performance and delivery would improve as a result.

Our inner critic often takes on the role of a heckler, constantly undermining us and making it harder for us to perform at our best. The key to transformation is to replace that heckling critic with an encouraging presence: an inner cheerleader.

When I began my journey of self-development and healing, I came across a book called *Solve for Happy* by Mo Gawdat. In it, Gawdat refers to his inner voice as 'Becky', personifying the self-critical voice that constantly undermined him. This helped him separate that voice from his true self. This resonated with me deeply – it reminded me of the first principle we discussed earlier: you are not your thoughts.

Instead of choosing a particular name, I simply called my inner critic 'the heckler'. I identified its qualities: judgemental, rude, demeaning and unforgiving. Then I visualised this character to help me further separate it from myself. In my mind, the heckler was a thick black cloud that created darkness wherever it went.

Then I thought to myself, 'If we can identify an inner critic, why not identify and create a kinder character that helps to boost our self-esteem rather than destroy it?' I decided to personify mine as 'the cheerleader'. I gave her qualities like encouraging, understanding, forgiving and non-judgemental. I imagined her as a bright white light radiating warmth – something I often visualise when I meditate.

✏️ EXERCISE: PERSONIFY YOUR INNER VOICE

Take a moment now to think about how you see your inner heckler. Then, visualise your inner cheerleader. This could be someone else, or it could simply be a version of *you* – the best version of yourself.

The inner heckler
Name: ....
Qualities: ....
Visualisation: ....

The cheerleader
Name: ....
Qualities: ....
Visualisation: ....

Now that you have a clear image of your inner cheerleader, you can start calling on this supportive voice whenever your inner heckler starts making noise. Imagine how your cheerleader would speak to you – what would they say? If you're struggling to find the words, think about what you would say to a best friend or loved one. Sometimes I like to think about what I would say to my sisters, because I always want the absolute best for them.

On the next page are a few examples of how you can change your internal dialogue from that of the heckler to the cheerleader:

The Heckler	The Cheerleader
You failed your driving test, which means that *you're* a failure.	Most people don't pass their test on their first try – you will get there. You've got this!
You kept shaking during your presentation – how embarrassing. You looked so unprofessional.	No one would've noticed – and anyway, you delivered an interesting presentation and you tried your best, which is what counts.
You couldn't even finish your workout – you're so out of shape and lazy.	You showed up and did what you could today, and that's what matters. Progress takes time, and you're getting stronger every day. Keep it up – you're doing great!
You argued with your partner and now they probably think less of you. It'll never work.	Disagreements happen in every relationship, and it's how you handle them that matters. Being able to communicate through conflict is actually how you strengthen a relationship.

Some of you might be excited to start using this new way of speaking to yourself, while others may feel awkward or even silly. I get it – when I first started talking to myself like a cheerleader, it felt strange too. But through practice and consistency, I began to notice a shift in my thinking and, ultimately, in how I felt. I encourage you to stick with it, even if it feels uncomfortable at first. Visualise your inner cheerleader and let that voice overrule the heckler. Over time, the kinder voice will grow stronger, and the critical one will fade into the background. It won't disappear completely overnight, but, with patience and commitment, it will become quieter and far less influential. Imagine how freeing that will feel.

Remember: You have the power to choose which voice you listen to and which you allow to influence the way you feel.

FAQ:

Q: How can you tell the difference between your inner critic and healthy self-awareness of your shortcomings?
A: I was recently asked, 'Should you always ignore your inner critic? Isn't it good to sometimes push yourself to do better?'

It's true that our inner critic might have evolved to help us by pointing out areas for improvement, providing feedback that can help us grow. However, there's a significant difference between constructive self-awareness and being harshly critical of ourselves. It's healthy to recognise our areas for growth, but our inner critic often takes it too far, turning feedback into relentless self-attack.

Imagine you've submitted a piece of work at university, knowing it isn't up to your usual standards, and your grades confirm this:

- **Inner critic's voice:** 'You're such an idiot. It's typical of you to produce work like this.'
- **Self-aware voice:** 'Yes, I was right; this wasn't my best work. How can I learn from this? What can I do better next time? It's okay – it's not the end of the world.'

> The main difference lies in the energy behind the message. The inner critic's voice is fuelled by insecurity, shame and negativity, while self-awareness is rooted in compassion and a desire to grow. When feedback comes from a place of kindness, it motivates us to improve without tearing us down. **The energy you bring to self-reflection is what determines whether it becomes a tool for growth or a weapon against yourself.**

POSITIVE AFFIRMATIONS

Cultivating our inner cheerleader is one powerful strategy to help master our thoughts, but another equally effective tool is positive affirmations. Affirmations are simple yet powerful statements we can repeat to ourselves to override negative thinking and feed our subconscious with empowering, supportive thoughts.

Research has shown that using positive affirmations enhances both mental and physical performance. They also help to boost mood and improve our resilience to stress. For instance, MRI studies have found that practising self-affirmation activates the reward centres in the brain, producing feelings of pleasure and reward.[4] Another study found that participants who engaged in self-affirmation recovered more quickly from stressful situations.[5]

The key to affirmations is understanding that the brain doesn't automatically differentiate between what is true and what isn't. Neuroscience shows that when we hear or think something repeatedly, our brain begins to accept it as true, regardless of its actual validity. This is partly because the brain relies on patterns and repetition to form neural connections, making certain thoughts and beliefs feel more familiar and, therefore, more believable.

In practical terms, this means that if you tell yourself repeatedly that you are 'not good enough' or you 'always have the worst luck', your brain begins to accept these statements as facts, even if they are not objectively true. Conversely, if you repeatedly replace these negative affirmations with positive ones, such as 'I am enough' or 'good things always happen to me', then your brain will start to form new neural pathways, and we will accept these statements as truth.

AFFIRMATIONS ARE A WAY TO SIGNAL TO OUR SUBCONSCIOUS THAT WE ARE ENOUGH, JUST AS WE ARE.

Affirmations help redirect our focus from what we lack to what we already possess and reinforce the idea that we are deserving of love, success and happiness.

Some examples of positive affirmations include:

- I am confident in my abilities.
- I am enough, just as I am.
- I am worthy of unconditional love.
- I have so much to offer the world.
- I will do my best, and that is enough.
- I love the person that I am.
- I am proud of how far I have come.
- I can achieve anything I set my mind to.

Tips for using affirmations effectively

Using positive affirmations was one of the first tools I used when I began my manifestation practice and, over the years, I've discovered a few strategies that really help to embed them, which I've shared with you on the next page.

Repeat affirmations first thing in the morning

In those moments just after waking, your mind is in a theta brainwave state – a relaxed, semi-drowsy condition that makes it highly receptive to suggestion. This natural transition between sleep and wakefulness is an ideal time to introduce positive affirmations. By repeating affirmations like 'I am confident and capable' or 'I am motivated to work towards my goals' first thing in the morning, you can set a positive tone for the rest of your day.

Incorporate affirmations into your daily routines

Use affirmations during the routine activities you already do each day, like brushing your teeth, making your bed or preparing breakfast. This makes it easy to reinforce positive thinking without needing extra time. These moments are often when your mind is on autopilot, so repeating affirmations during these times can also help replace automatic negative thoughts with positive ones.

Disrupt the inner critic with affirmations

When you catch your inner heckler trying to take over, you can use an affirmation to interrupt it. For instance, if you start thinking, 'You're going to mess this up; everyone will think you're incompetent,' right before a presentation, replace it with an affirmation like 'I am well-prepared and confident in my abilities'. This practice stops negative thoughts in their tracks while reinforcing a positive belief that helps you perform better.

Create personal affirmations

Make affirmations more meaningful by tailoring them to your needs. Identify a limiting belief and turn it into a positive statement. For example, if you often think, 'I'm so nervous about this exam,' turn it into 'I am ready for this challenge'. Or if you worry about meeting new people, affirm, 'I am kind and personable, and people enjoy meeting me'. By transforming a negative thought into a positive one, you train your mind to focus on optimistic possibilities.

Fall asleep to an affirmation meditation
The moments before sleep are another powerful opportunity to shape your subconscious mind, as your brain returns to a theta state. Try an affirmation meditation – guided affirmations repeated over calming music – just before bed. As you listen, the affirmations replace negative thoughts with empowering ones. The best part? You don't need to do anything but press play and fall asleep. You can find my affirmation meditations at www.roxienafousi.com or look for similar content for free on YouTube.

> **Note:** Whether you say affirmations aloud or just in your mind, it's normal to feel a bit self-conscious at first. If saying something positive to yourself feels uncomfortable, consider it a sign of how much you need it! Like anything, the more you practise, the more natural it will feel.

FINAL WORDS

The journey to becoming the most confident and empowered version of yourself begins with mastering your thoughts. Our thoughts shape how we feel, drive our behaviour and form the beliefs we hold about who we are. They have incredible power over our lives – power we can learn to reclaim.

For years, I couldn't go a single day without tearing myself apart. I would leave every room convinced that no one liked me, and I would lie in bed at night replaying every mistake, real or imagined, from the day. My inner critic – the heckler – felt like an unwelcome guest who refused to leave. It was exhausting, and it consumed so much of my energy.

But everything began to change once I found the right tools to break free. The first step was awareness: recognising my inner critic, noticing when it was loudest and understanding where those thoughts were coming from. Next, I learned to challenge my negative thoughts – interviewing them, questioning their validity and identifying the cognitive biases that fuelled them. Each time I confronted my negative thoughts, I stripped away some of their power.

Replacing the heckler with an inner cheerleader became a powerful antidote to my self-criticism. Personifying a kind, supportive voice inside my mind gave me the encouragement I desperately needed. And then, there were positive affirmations – simple yet transformative. Repeating affirmations like 'I am capable of anything I put my mind to' and 'I am deserving of love and success' rewired my brain to focus on empowering beliefs rather than dwelling on self-doubt.

Slowly but surely, these practices shifted my mindset. The change was subtle at first, but one day I realised that I had more mental space and more energy because I was no longer exhausting myself with constant criticism. Life became infinitely easier when I replaced self-judgement with self-compassion.

My inner critic still tries to speak up, especially in moments when I'm overwhelmed, tired or triggered by old insecurities. But now, it doesn't spiral or linger in the way it used to. I have the strength to say, 'No, we're not doing that anymore,' and replace those thoughts with something kind and uplifting.

Mastering your thoughts is perhaps the most important part of this journey, and it's also one of the hardest. It requires dedication, patience and the willingness to unlearn years of negative thinking. You may stumble along the way – there will be setbacks and moments when your inner critic seems impossible to quiet. But healing is not a straight path. Don't be discouraged if progress feels slow. Keep going.

Think about it like this: if we have the power to convince ourselves that we aren't enough, we also have the power to convince ourselves that we absolutely are. Knowing the influence our mind holds should excite you – imagine how radically your life will transform when you learn to harness that power in the right way. You will feel free and you will *thrive*.

STEP 2

ACT WITH INTENTION

Actions speak louder than words.

ROXIE NAFOUSI — CONFIDENCE

Our actions are a powerful way to communicate our feelings, intentions and beliefs. For example, making a coffee for your partner in the morning can be a way of saying 'I love you' or helping a friend move house can show 'I care about you'. Similarly, our daily actions, habits and behaviours send important messages to ourselves about our values, capabilities and self-worth.

THE CHOICES WE MAKE EVERY DAY SHAPE OUR SELF-PERCEPTION AND DIRECTLY INFLUENCE OUR CONFIDENCE. OUR ACTIONS, BIG AND SMALL, EITHER BUILD US UP OR BREAK US DOWN.

Before I began my healing journey, my self-esteem was on the floor, and the way I treated myself mirrored that. I was committed to habits that kept me trapped in a cycle of shame and self-loathing: smoking, procrastinating, sleeping late, scrolling excessively on social media and drinking. I had little to no self-discipline, was extremely unmotivated and easily distracted. Even when I tried to be 'healthy', like exercising or going on health kicks, it always came from a place of punishment rather than nourishment.

Negative habits function a lot like negative self-talk. My daily actions sent a clear message to myself: 'I don't love you. I don't respect you. I don't care about your future.' Every time I hit the snooze button or woke up with another hangover, I fed my inner critic – the voice telling me I'd never amount to anything. I felt stuck in a destructive cycle, where low self-esteem led to negative habits, and those habits only deepened my lack of confidence.

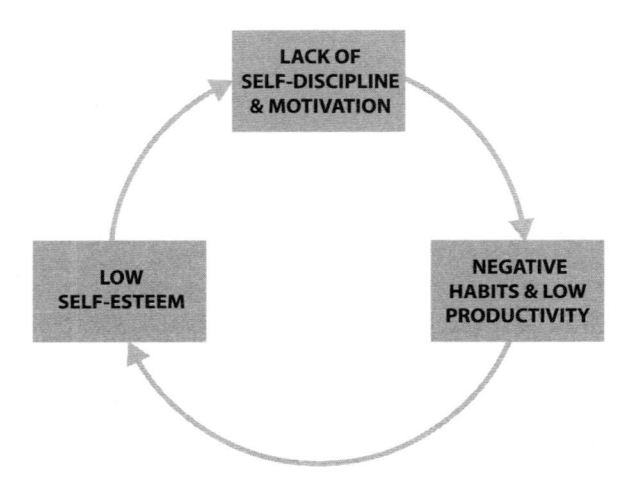

```
      LACK OF
  SELF-DISCIPLINE
   & MOTIVATION

LOW                    NEGATIVE
SELF-ESTEEM         HABITS & LOW
                     PRODUCTIVITY
```

I know how hard it is to break out of this cycle. When confidence is low, the idea of changing your habits can feel overwhelming. And it's not just a matter of lacking willpower – there's a deeper force at play: **subconscious resistance**.

Our subconscious mind craves comfort and familiarity, even if the familiar is harmful. It doesn't differentiate between good or bad – it just clings to what it knows. That's why we often stick to negative habits; on a subconscious level, they feel safe. This is also why we delay making changes, telling ourselves we'll quit drinking 'next week' or start a diet 'on Monday'. Deep down, the unfamiliar feels threatening.

Even if we muster the motivation to start something positive, our subconscious often pulls us back to old habits – *in other words, we self-sabotage*. I remember how many times I would decide to quit sugar. I'd do it for a week, only to 'celebrate' my success with a huge bag of pick 'n' mix, undoing all my progress. Looking back, I can see that my subconscious was just trying to bring me back to what felt familiar.

Here's the good news: awareness is the key to breaking this cycle. When you understand that your mind is simply trying to keep you safe, you can start making conscious choices to override these old patterns. You don't need rock-solid confidence to begin – just a willingness to take one small step at a time. Every positive action, no matter how small, starts to build new habits and shift the cycle in your favour.

Now, I'm going to guide you through two key strategies that will help you create lasting change:

1. Creating new habits.
2. Cultivating self-discipline.

CREATING NEW HABITS

HABIT (noun): *A settled or regular tendency or practice.* (*Oxford Languages*)

Before we introduce new habits into our lives, let's first step back and evaluate our existing habits. By understanding the impact of our current behaviours, we can make more informed decisions about which new habits to adopt and which old ones to modify or eliminate.

✎ EXERCISE: CARRY OUT A HABIT AUDIT

Use the steps below to identify which habits are currently benefiting you and helping you move closer to your goals and the person you want to become, and which are holding you back.

Step 1

In a notebook or journal, write down every single habit you have, from when you wake up to when you go to bed. Next to each one, note whether you do it every day, multiple times a week or multiple times a month. Your list might look a bit like this (but it will likely be a lot longer!):

Pressing 'snooze' on alarm – multiple times a week
Brushing teeth – every day
Vaping – every day
Making my bed – most days
Yoga class – multiple times a month
Procrastinate at work by scrolling Instagram – every day

Step 2

Once you have your full list of habits, grab a couple of coloured highlighters (or simply draw symbols if you don't have highlighters).

Use one colour (or a smiley face) for the habits that serve you – those you know are good for you. If you're unsure, think about which habits make you feel healthy and in control. Which habits would you still like to have next year? Which would you recommend to someone you love? Go through your list and mark all the habits you consider 'positive'. Think of these habits as being on the same team as the inner cheerleader we met in Step 1: Master Your Thoughts (see page 36).

Next, use another colour (or a sad face) for the habits that aren't serving you. To clarify, ask yourself: which habits do you hope to stop by next year? Which could have negative health consequences? Which would you advise a friend against? Which habits make you feel worse afterwards or amplify your inner critic? Mark these habits clearly.

> **Note**: Some habits may not clearly fit into either category, and that's okay. For example, coffee might be a 'bad habit' for one person if it causes anxiety, but an enjoyable part of your day for another. Reflect on what each habit means to you. It's perfectly fine to leave some habits unmarked.

> Remember, there's a difference between a habit and an addiction. If the idea of reducing or eliminating a behaviour feels overwhelming, or if you feel out of control, don't hesitate to seek help. I've struggled with addiction myself, and I know how hard it can be to admit it – but reaching out is one of the bravest things you can do. Consider talking to someone you trust, visiting your GP or contacting a support organisation like actiononaddiction.org.uk.

Now that you've identified your 'habit baseline' – what's working for you and what's holding you back – it's time to start making changes.

Here are my top tips for creating healthy habits.

Go slow

I once had a client who came to me wanting more stability and balance. He told me that everything in his life felt extreme. He was either working long hours, neglecting his health and partying all weekend, or he was on an extreme wellness kick – staying in every night to avoid temptation and going to retreats every weekend. He wanted change, but he was going about it in the wrong way.

For change to last, we have to integrate new habits into our real-world routines, making them work around our jobs, commitments and families.

Some people might feel energised by the idea of a complete lifestyle overhaul – and if that sounds like you, I wouldn't want to discourage you from giving it a try (it does work for some people). However, in my experience, making several major changes all at once can be tough to sustain. For example, if you go from not exercising at all to going to the gym five times a week, you might end up feeling physically burned out and be more likely to quit. Or if, like my client, you stop going out to see friends in an attempt to prioritise health, you'll likely end up rebelling against the loneliness that it creates.

Self-discipline shouldn't feel like punishment; it needs to be manageable and feel achievable. Otherwise, you risk losing momentum. This is important because giving up can damage your confidence by eroding your self-trust. It sends the message: 'I can't keep my promises to myself.' This is why finding ways to minimise the risk of quitting is so important.

So, instead of a complete overhaul, let's start small:

Reflect on your habit audit and choose just one or two habits from your 'good' list that you'd like to strengthen, and one or two from your 'bad' list that you'd like to reduce or eliminate. Focusing on a small number of habits to change allows you to direct your energy effectively and increases your chances of success. For instance, if excessive screen time is an issue, limit Instagram scrolling to 15 minutes during work hours, or if you want to exercise more often, add one extra workout class each week.

After successfully sticking to these changes for a week, introduce another 'good' habit to build on, and further reduce or eliminate another 'bad' habit. The advantage of this approach is that the sense of pride and accomplishment you'll feel from honouring your commitment will make it easier to stay motivated as you tackle the next habit on your list.

. IT IS INCREDIBLY EMPOWERING TO DO THE THINGS YOU TELL YOURSELF YOU ARE GOING TO DO.

> **Note:** Be thoughtful about the habits you choose. Visualise the most confident version of yourself and ask: which habits would that version of me commit to? Remember, your habits need to work for you and fit into your life – they should feel good to you! Avoid choosing habits just because they sound like 'good' habits or because others recommend them. For example, you don't need to journal just because people say it's helpful. If writing isn't enjoyable for you, that's totally fine. The point isn't what you do, it's that you're doing things that make you feel good and, most importantly, that you're sticking to them.

If you start a habit and realise it's not working for you, feel free to adjust. Just aim to replace it with something else, rather than letting go of positive change altogether.

> ### REPLACE BAD HABITS WITH GOOD ONES
>
> When reducing or eliminating a 'bad' habit, it can be helpful to replace it with a positive one. Our brains are wired to seek rewards, and if you simply remove a habit without replacing it with something equally satisfying, you may find it harder to stick to your change. By replacing a negative behaviour with a positive one, you create a new reward system that supports your goals and strengthens your resolve.
>
> For example, if you want to cut down on an unhealthy habit like reaching for sugary snacks, replace it with a healthy alternative that you also enjoy – like fresh fruit or nuts. Over time, your brain will begin to associate the new habit with a similar sense of satisfaction, making it easier to let go of the old one.

Bookend your day

A powerful way to create a consistent routine is to 'bookend' your day with healthy habits – committing to a few positive actions in the morning and in the evening. For me, this means that, even among the chaos and unpredictability of the day, I know I can start and end it in an empowering and grounding way.

Morning routine
I recently had the pleasure of interviewing Jay Shetty for my podcast *RISE with Roxie*, and I was so inspired by what he shared

about the importance of morning routines. Jay said, 'Our days are full of uncertainty; we don't know exactly what is coming, but we can know how we will start the day. It becomes like an armour that we put on to help us as we step into the unknown.' I loved this analogy of a morning routine as armour – something that shields us from the stresses and unpredictability of daily life.

A morning routine is more than just a set of actions; it's a form of preparation that empowers us to face whatever comes our way with greater resilience and confidence. It's about starting the day with intention and supporting ourselves mentally, emotionally and physically.

Morning habits could include:

- **Making your bed:** A simple task that gives you a sense of accomplishment straight away.
- **Repeating positive affirmations:** Reprogramming your mindset with empowering beliefs (see page 43).
- **Implementing a skincare routine:** Taking a few minutes for self-care and nurturing your body.
- **Drinking your morning coffee or tea mindfully, without distractions:** Enjoying a moment of calm and presence.
- **Preparing and eating a nutritious breakfast:** Fuelling your body with nourishing foods that sustain energy.
- **Taking your supplements:** Supporting your physical health and well-being.
- **Doing breathwork/meditation:** Cultivating mindfulness and reducing stress.
- **Journaling:** Reflecting on your thoughts and setting intentions for the day.
- **Doing Pilates or yoga:** Engaging in gentle, mindful movement to awaken your body.
- **Taking a walk in nature:** Connecting with the outdoors to boost mood and gain clarity.

- **Stretching:** Warming up your muscles and easing any morning stiffness.
- **Having a cold shower:** Invigorating your body and boosting circulation.
- **Reading or listening to something insightful:** Starting your day with inspiration and knowledge.
- **Making a to-do list:** Organising your priorities and tasks to feel more in control.

MY MORNING ROUTINE

Use the space below to jot down the morning habits that could support you in starting your day with intention and purpose. Note the time on the left and the habit on the right.

_____ : ....
_____ : ....
_____ : ....
_____ : ....
_____ : ....
_____ : ....

Evening routine

Evening routines are just as crucial as morning ones, even though they often don't receive the same attention. The primary purpose of an evening routine is to help you unwind and prepare your mind and body for a restful night's sleep. When we're well-rested, we're much better equipped to put our best foot forward and show up as our most vibrant, resilient and energised selves.

Sleep plays a significant role in our confidence. Lack of sleep has been linked to increased feelings of anger, frustration and sadness – emotions that can undermine our sense of self-worth.[1] In fact, a 2013 study found that individuals who slept fewer than six hours a night reported lower levels of optimism and self-esteem compared to those who enjoyed seven to eight hours of sleep.[2] This shows how important a good night's sleep is, not just for our physical health but also for our emotional well-being and confidence.

Everyone's sleep needs are different – some of us are naturally better sleepers, while others may find it easier to function on fewer hours. Knowing your own baseline is important, but there are still many steps we can all take to give ourselves the best chance for a restful night. Here are a few simple evening habits that can make a big difference:

- **Dim the lights a few hours before bed:** Not only does this create a calming atmosphere that activates the parasympathetic nervous system (the part of your brain associated with rest), but dimmer lights also work with your circadian rhythm to send the signal to your brain that it's night-time and time for sleep.
- **If worrying often keeps you awake, try journaling in the evening:** Research has found that bedtime writing can reduce sleep onset latency (the time it takes to fall asleep).[3] You might choose to 'brain dump' all your worries onto the page, or reflect on the day and offer yourself some compassionate advice, as if you were writing a letter to a friend. If you're unsure where to start, here are some helpful journaling prompts:

  ○ What went well today?
  ○ What did I find challenging today?
  ○ What has been playing on my mind?
  ○ What reassuring words can I give to myself about my worries?
  ○ What am I grateful for?
  ○ What am I looking forward to tomorrow?

Other evening habits to try include:

- **Stretching or practising Yin Yoga:** Releasing any tension stored in your body.
- **Drinking herbal tea:** Opting for calming teas like chamomile or lavender.
- **Listening to relaxing music or white noise:** Creating a peaceful atmosphere.
- **Repeating positive affirmations:** Ending the day with self-kindness (see page 44).
- **Meditating:** Clearing your mind in preparation for sleep.
- **Taking a warm bath:** Soothing your muscles and relaxing.
- **Lighting candles or using aromatherapy:** Creating a calming environment.
- **Putting your phone on airplane mode:** Reducing digital distractions.
- **Reading a book:** Helping your mind transition from active thought to rest.
- **Listening to a sleep story or guided meditation:** Allowing your mind to relax and drift off.

MY EVENING ROUTINE

Use the space below to note down any evening habits that will help you to unwind and get a restful night's sleep.

_____ : ....
_____ : ....
_____ : ....
_____ : ....
_____ : ....
_____ : ....

Stack your habits

James Clear, in his book *Atomic Habits*, introduced the concept of 'habit stacking', a technique that involves pairing a new habit with an existing one to make it easier to incorporate into your daily routine. This approach leverages the existing patterns in your day, allowing the new habit to become a natural extension of something you're already doing.

To use this approach, think about the moments in your day that are already part of your routine – the things you do almost on autopilot, like waiting for the kettle to boil in the morning or commuting to work. You might also think about the good habits you noted in your habit audit earlier. Then consider how you can attach a new habit to these pre-existing actions, making it easier for the new habit to become a natural part of your daily routine.

As Clear explains, 'The reason habit stacking works so well is that your current habits are already built into your brain. You have patterns and behaviours that have been reinforced over years. By linking your new habits to a cycle that is already ingrained, you make it more likely that you'll stick with the new habit.'

Here are some examples of habit stacking, but I encourage you to create your own, working with your existing daily routine:

- **While you have your morning coffee** → Write down your to-do list for the day.
- **When you take your regular medication** → Take your supplements.
- **On your morning commute** → Listen to a podcast that teaches you something valuable.
- **After finishing lunch** → Take a short walk and enjoy some fresh air.
- **After changing into your pyjamas** → Write down three things you accomplished or are proud of that day.

Track your progress and celebrate

There's a reason parents/caregivers and teachers use star charts to encourage good behaviour in children – the satisfaction of earning a gold star creates a positive association by activating the brain's reward centre, releasing dopamine and making it more likely the behaviour will be repeated. The same principle can work for us: writing down the habits we want to complete each day and checking them off as we go creates a similar sense of accomplishment and reward.

Consider using a habit tracker to provide a visual representation of your progress. This could be as simple as marking off days on a calendar, creating a chart in a notebook or using one of the many habit tracker apps available.

Then, reinforce positive change by celebrating your progress. When we actively celebrate our wins – no matter how small – we create a positive association that motivates us to continue our journey. The act of self-recognition tells us, 'I see your efforts, and I'm proud of you.'

Celebrating progress doesn't require grand gestures. It could be as simple as enjoying a candlelit bath, reflecting for five minutes on the positive benefits of sticking to your habit or ordering your favourite takeaway for dinner. These moments of self-celebration boost your self-worth and remind you of how far you've come, making it more likely that you'll stay engaged with your habits.

Research shows that even small wins can be incredibly motivating, creating a sense of momentum that keeps us moving forward.[4] This phenomenon is sometimes called the 'progress principle'. According to Harvard Business School professor Teresa Amabile, making progress in meaningful work is one of the most powerful motivators. Each step forward, no matter how small, reinforces our motivation and boosts our confidence, helping us tackle even bigger challenges over time.

Make it a habit to celebrate yourself regularly. Notice your efforts and honour your progress.

Acknowledge the domino effect

One of the most powerful aspects of forming new, positive habits is their tendency to create a domino effect. Take, for example, the habit of getting up early. Many successful people – from Michelle Obama to Apple CEO Tim Cook – attribute part of their success to waking up early. By getting up even an hour earlier, you give yourself extra time to do something beneficial, such as exercising, meditating or preparing a healthy breakfast. That one change can set the tone for a healthier and more productive day.

Many habits have similar ripple effects. For instance, a 2015 study found that people who established a regular exercise routine naturally began to gravitate towards healthier diets, such as eating more fruits and vegetables.[5]

As we start to experience the benefits of new habits, we gain momentum, making it easier to adopt additional positive changes. Think of good habits like a line of dominoes – knocking one over sets off a chain reaction that leads to another, and then another. Trust me: once you initiate one positive change, others will follow more effortlessly.

Be compassionate and flexible

Self-compassion is crucial on this journey. If you're too hard on yourself after setbacks, you're more likely to give up altogether. Remember, the goal isn't a perfect routine every single day. I don't meditate or journal every day – I just aim to do it most days. When I miss a day, I don't beat myself up about it; I just get back to it as soon as I can. Being overly rigid can be as counterproductive as having no routine at all, as it leaves no room for flexibility, growth or unexpected opportunities.

What I would say, however, is that there is a fine line between knowing when you need to rest and when you need to give yourself a kick up the backside – and only you know where that line is. Setbacks are normal and part of the journey. If you slip up, don't dwell on it. Instead, refocus on your goals and keep moving forward. And, if you find that certain habits are harder to change than expected, or that your goals need adjusting, don't be afraid to reassess and modify your plan.

THE ULTIMATE GOAL IS PROGRESS, NOT PERFECTION.

FAQ

Q: I have kids – how do I make time for new habits when my days are already full enough as it is?

A: First of all, I hear you! It's not always possible to exercise or spend 15 minutes journaling in the morning when you have to do the school run and then rush to the office, and you might feel so exhausted by the evening that you don't have the energy to read or do a Yin Yoga class. My advice would be *not to put too much pressure on yourself*. Only commit to habits that can genuinely work around your life and schedule. Good habits should never feel like punishment. They should add to your life – and make it feel better, not harder.

Think carefully about the moments in your day where you *could* integrate some time for positive change – even if it's just one small thing. If you do the school drop-off on foot, could you take the longer route home and listen to a self-development podcast? When the kids are in bed, could you swap your evening Instagram scroll for a mindful meditation?

You could also get your family involved in your healthy habits. Perhaps you could integrate a gratitude practice into your evening dinners: ask everyone for one thing they were grateful for that day. You could also start the day with affirmations, for both yourself and your partner/kids. Not only does this allow you to build healthier habits into your day, it also sets a great example, teaching them the value of these habits too – helping to boost their confidence as well.

CULTIVATING SELF-DISCIPLINE

We've explored how to identify and establish positive habits, now we need to make them stick. *Enter self-discipline.* Without self-discipline, even the best intentions can quickly lose their momentum.

Think of self-discipline as the quiet, consistent force that keeps you moving forward, even when motivation fades or life gets in the way. It's this discipline that ultimately builds confidence – each time you honour your commitment to yourself, you reinforce the belief that you are reliable and capable.

Self-discipline isn't about punishment or strict control; it's an expression of self-love and self-respect. Practising self-discipline tells us that our goals, health and well-being are worth the effort. It's a conscious decision to prioritise what truly matters, even when it's easier to give in to short-term desires or old habits. Self-discipline is about making choices that align with our long-term goals and staying committed because we believe we are worthy of a life filled with joy, success and love.

SELF-DISCIPLINE IS A FORM OF SELF-LOVE.

Self-discipline is like a muscle – the more you use it, the stronger it gets. When we consistently make empowering choices, whether it's sticking to a fitness routine, dedicating time to personal growth or following through on our commitments, we send a powerful message to ourselves: 'I value my well-being and am willing to put in the effort to create the life I desire.' These repeated affirmations, communicated through action, build self-trust and self-respect, reinforcing our belief in our ability to achieve our goals.

Self-discipline isn't just about willpower; it's about having the right tools and mindset to navigate challenges. These challenges can range from a stressful day that tempts you to revert to old comforting habits, to a lack of motivation that makes it difficult to stick to your new routines. Here are some tips to help you when that happens:

- **Identify potential obstacles:** Start by identifying the situations, triggers or emotions that might cause you to slip back into old habits. Are there certain times of day, environments or social settings where you're more likely to face temptation? Understanding your triggers helps you prepare for them.
- **Create a support system:** Let those close to you know about the changes you're trying to make and ask for their support. Whether it's joining you for a workout or encouraging you to stick to your goals, having others on your side can make a big difference. You might also consider joining a group or community with similar goals. This could be an online forum, a local club or a class – being part of a supportive network provides motivation and accountability.

- **Practise positive self-talk:** Use positive self-talk to encourage yourself when you feel like giving up. Remind yourself of the benefits you'll gain by persevering.
- **Remember your why:** When motivation starts to fall, remind yourself of the bigger picture – the deeper reasons you set these goals in the first place.

Cultivating self-discipline, and committing to habits that make you feel good, are an important part of the confidence journey. They provide you with a constant feeling of accomplishment and help you to build self-trust and self-respect.

Productivity breeds productivity

One of my favourite sayings is, 'If you want something done, ask a busy person.' I've found this to be true in my life; when I'm busiest, I'm often at my most efficient, driven and motivated. Have you ever noticed how much easier it is to keep going once you're already in motion?

This isn't just a coincidence – there's a scientific reason behind it. Productivity activates the reward centre in your brain, releasing dopamine – a chemical that makes you feel good and reinforces the desire to keep being productive. This is why, when you're crossing things off your to-do list, you often feel a sense of satisfaction that drives you to do even more.

On the other hand, when you have too much free time, it can be difficult to get started on anything. You may have found that a day spent in front of the TV or staying inside on a cold, rainy day can leave you feeling lethargic and unmotivated to tackle even the simplest of tasks. I have often said that **there is nothing more tiring than doing nothing**. Without momentum, it's easy to fall into procrastination and feel overwhelmed by tasks that normally wouldn't faze you.

To keep yourself in motion, it's important to stay engaged with meaningful activities, even if it's just sticking to your morning and evening habits. These small actions help you maintain momentum and create a positive cycle of accomplishment. But remember, productivity isn't about being constantly busy or overloading your schedule – that's a one-way ticket to burnout. Instead, it's about making the most of your time, focusing on what matters to you and creating a positive cycle of progress that will help you achieve a deeper sense of accomplishment.

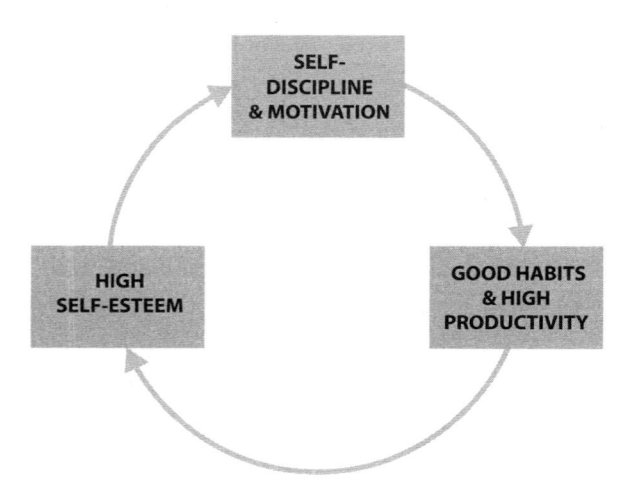

```
        SELF-
     DISCIPLINE
    & MOTIVATION

HIGH                GOOD HABITS
SELF-ESTEEM          & HIGH
                   PRODUCTIVITY
```

Do that thing you've been putting off

We all have those tasks lingering on our to-do lists – the ones we keep pushing aside because they seem tedious, time-consuming or just plain annoying. Whether it's applying for a new passport, cleaning out the fridge or finally selling those clothes you no longer wear, these tasks have a way of hanging over us, draining our mental energy even when we try to ignore them.

I want you to get into the practice of doing those things you've been putting off and getting them done before they begin to loom over you. Here's how I approach this: in my mind, I fast forward to how good I will feel once the task is complete, that feeling of pure relief. **Visualise the sense of relief washing over you – like drinking an ice-cold glass of water when you're thirsty.** That feeling of satisfaction is powerful, and it's exactly what awaits you once you get that task done.

To make it even easier, try **reframing your mindset** around the task. Instead of thinking, 'Ugh, I have to do this,' change it to, 'I'm so excited for this to be done.' Focus on the reward that comes with completing the task – the lightness you'll feel once it's off your plate. By shifting your perspective from dread to excitement, you make the task less daunting and more achievable – and you'll be another step closer to cultivating self-discipline and creating lasting change.

FINAL WORDS

In this step, we've explored the powerful connection between our actions and our self-perception. Every choice we make carries the potential to shape our confidence, self-worth and, ultimately, our future.

By choosing habits that align with the person we want to become and cultivating self-discipline, we can transform not only how we feel, but also how we see ourselves and our potential.

Remember, this isn't about perfection – it's about progress. Every step forward, no matter how small, is a step towards becoming the most empowered, authentic version of ourselves. When we take deliberate, positive actions, we begin to trust ourselves more deeply and believe in our ability to create the life we truly want.

STEP 3

STOP TRYING TO BE LIKED BY EVERYBODY

Stop trying to be liked by everyone; you don't even like everyone.

ROXIE NAFOUSI — CONFIDENCE

Like many people, I spent much of my life longing for acceptance. In the Introduction, I spoke about my struggle to fit in; from an early age, I learned to change my behaviour or find inventive ways to try to be liked. For example, I remember how my mum would always pack my lunchbox with chocolate and sweets, and I'd give them away during break times, hoping it might make the other kids include me in their games. Later, when I started getting pocket money at 12, I'd spend it buying lunch for classmates, trying to offer something of value because I didn't believe I was enough as I was.

Fast forward to my twenties, and my desperation to be liked had only become stronger. I found myself willing to compromise on my values, do things I didn't want to do or pretend to be someone I wasn't, just to be seen as 'fun' or 'cool'. This is how my destructive relationship with partying, drugs and unhealthy romantic relationships began. I constantly sought validation from others, especially men, relying on them to make me feel good about myself. My confidence was hanging by a thread, and it was entirely dependent on how other people viewed and treated me. I know that my story is far from unique. Most of us share a deep desire to be liked and loved by others.

Before we go any further, I want you to understand that seeking approval from others is natural. **It's a fundamental human**

need to want to belong. Psychologists have long recognised this as an intrinsic part of our social nature. As we discussed earlier, Maslow's Hierarchy of Needs places 'love and belonging' just below 'self-esteem' on the pyramid, showing that when we feel loved, respected and valued, it becomes easier to build our self-esteem (see page 8).

There's another reason why we care about what others think: we are inherently social beings who evolved to rely on one another for survival. Thousands of years ago, humans travelled in groups for safety and protection. Our ancestors needed to be well-liked so that their peers would care for them, and they had to be attuned to social cues to avoid danger. For them, acceptance wasn't just about belonging – it was essential for survival.

Over time, this need for acceptance has shifted. It's no longer about physical safety; instead, we often rely on social approval to define our self-worth. Our desire to be accepted and liked now comes at a great cost: we lose sight of who we truly are and struggle to build a strong internal foundation for confidence to grow. Instead of using social approval as a tool to navigate a dangerous world, we now use it to validate our existence and measure our value. This shift – from external safety to internal validation – has led many of us to believe that our worth is entirely tied to how others perceive us.

HOW THE NEED FOR SOCIAL ACCEPTANCE DEVELOPS THROUGHOUT CHILDHOOD

Ages 4–5: Children become more socially aware and start seeking approval from parents/caregivers, teachers and peers. They might show a desire to fit in by copying behaviours, interests or language from those around them.

> **Ages 6–11:** Children start forming close friendships and may feel pressure to conform to group norms in order to be liked. They also start to compare themselves to their peers, becoming more aware of differences and similarities.
>
> **Ages 12–18:** The desire for social acceptance peaks during the teenage years. Teens become highly sensitive to peer opinions, and may engage in more risky behaviours to gain approval and acceptance.

THE CONSEQUENCES OF OUR NEED TO BE LIKED

Our need to be liked can have extremely detrimental effects on our self-worth, confidence and the quality of our lives. Here are a few ways it impacts us:

People-pleasing behaviour

The desire to be liked often manifests as people-pleasing behaviour, where we prioritise others' needs and opinions over our own. This can result in saying 'yes' when we want to say 'no', overcommitting ourselves and neglecting our own boundaries and well-being. Over time, this erodes our self-respect and can leave us feeling exhausted, resentful and unfulfilled, as we lose touch with our own desires and needs.

Fear of rejection

A deep fear of rejection can develop from the need to be liked, leading us to avoid situations where we might face criticism or disapproval. This fear can hold us back from taking risks, pursuing our goals or expressing our true selves. We may stay in unfulfilling jobs or relationships simply because they provide a sense of acceptance, even if they don't align with the person we want to become or the life we want to lead.

Loss of authenticity

When we are overly concerned with being liked, we may alter our behaviour, opinions or appearance to fit in with those around us. This constant adaptation can lead to a loss of authenticity, where we no longer feel connected to our true selves. Over time, this disconnect can make us feel empty or lost, as we struggle to remember who we really are and what we genuinely want from life.

Stunted personal growth

The need to be liked can prevent us from growing and evolving as individuals. When we focus too much on others' opinions, we may avoid challenging ourselves or stepping out of our comfort zones, fearing that doing so might lead to disapproval. This avoidance can stifle our personal development, leaving us stuck in patterns of behaviour that no longer serve us, and preventing us from reaching our full potential.

Increased anxiety and stress

Continually seeking approval can create a heightened state of anxiety. When we constantly worry about others' perceptions, it affects our mental health, increasing stress levels and leading to emotional burnout.

HOW IMAGINED PERCEPTIONS AFFECT OUR IDENTITY

There's a powerful quote by the psychologist Charles Cooley that often comes to mind: **'I am not who I think I am, and I am not what you think I am. I am what I think you think I am.'** It's a bit of a tongue-twister, but I love its message because it highlights a common trap: **our tendency to base our worth on how we assume others perceive us.**

In practice, this means we're constantly trying to interpret how others see us, using those imagined perceptions as a mirror for our own value. It's not about what others *actually* think, but what we *believe* they think – and, often, those imagined judgements carry more weight than our own feelings or opinions.

Take my client, for example, who is a talented artist and takes pride in the respect people have for her work. She recently had a gallery opening, showcasing some of her most personal pieces, but the turnout wasn't what she hoped for, and fewer pieces sold compared to her previous shows. Even though she once felt deeply proud of this collection, she quickly adopted a belief that others didn't see value in it – and that perception overshadowed her original pride. She began to think of her art as a failure, without considering that other factors, like the timing of the event or external circumstances, could have influenced that outcome. The anxiety and second-guessing took over, stifling the creativity that was once fuelled by passion and self-expression, as she became consumed by how she thought others judged her.

This isn't just about my client – many of us do the same thing. We adopt the judgements we *assume* others hold about us and use them to shape our self-image. If we assume others don't respect or understand us, it can shake our confidence and limit how we show up in the world. Maybe you don't get up and dance at a wedding because you're worried that everyone will think you look ridiculous. Or perhaps you don't post about your small business because you fear your friends will think it's silly. **These imagined judgements become a mirror, reflecting back a distorted image of ourselves that holds us back from fully expressing who we are.**

THE PROBLEM WITH EXTERNAL VALIDATION

VALIDATION (noun): *Recognition or affirmation that a person or their feelings or opinions are valid or worthwhile.* (*Oxford Languages*)

Research has shown that receiving social approval and verbal praise triggers dopamine release in the brain, creating feelings of pleasure and motivation.[1] Social media validation has a similar effect. A study by the University of California, Los Angeles (UCLA) found that teenagers who received a high number of 'likes' on their photos experienced increased activity in brain areas linked to dopamine release.[2]

However, the problem with these dopamine hits is that they're fleeting. They provide a quick, temporary boost – like the short-lived high you get from eating something sweet – but they fade just as quickly. This is why we often find ourselves seeking validation repeatedly, in the hope of recapturing that fleeting feeling of satisfaction.

Have you ever noticed that a compliment can sometimes feel like it goes in one ear and out the other? For example, if your partner often tells you how talented you are at your job, but, deep down, you're plagued by self-doubt and feel like an imposter, their words might give you a momentary boost. However, that reassurance quickly fades, and you're straight back to questioning your abilities. Why? Because no matter how many times someone else praises you, it won't truly stick unless you begin to believe it yourself.

Think of external validation as a burst of wind filling a sail. It can propel you forward, but without a solid boat beneath you, there's nothing to keep you afloat. The boat represents your internal validation – the structure that provides stability and keeps you steady no matter what. The wind, like praise from others, can help you move faster, but it's the boat that keeps you from sinking. To move forward, you need a strong boat to rely on, even when the wind dies down.

We've already discussed the importance of developing your inner cheerleader (see page 36), and we'll dive deeper into building internal validation in the upcoming chapters, especially in Step 5: Celebrate Yourself. But, for now, I encourage you to start reflecting on who you seek external validation from and why. Remember, self-awareness is the first step towards meaningful change.

✏️ EXERCISE: WHO IS VALIDATING YOU?

To better understand your need for validation, take a moment to reflect on the people whose opinions matter most to you.

1. **List the sources:** In a notebook or journal, write down all the people whose opinions you care about most. Is it someone you're dating? Your partner? Your parents/caregivers? Friends? Colleagues? *Or perhaps it's strangers on social media?*
2. **Ask yourself:**
   - **Do these people truly want the best for you?** Are they supportive in a way that aligns with your own values and growth, or do they impose their own expectations on you?
   - **Do they accept you as you are, without expecting you to change?** Do they value you for who you are at your core, or does their love/admiration seem to come with conditions?

- **Is the validation mutual or is it one-sided?**
  Are you investing just as much in them as they are in you, or do you find yourself constantly seeking their approval without getting much back?
- **How do you feel when they validate you?**
  Does their affirmation genuinely uplift you or does it feel like a momentary high that leaves you craving more?
- **How do you feel when they don't validate you?**
  Does it trigger a cascade of self-doubt, affect your mood or make you question your self-worth?
- **What actions or decisions would you make if their opinions were taken out of the equation?**
  How much of your current behaviour is shaped by the need for their approval?
3. **Reflect:** Reflect on which relationships are nurturing your self-worth and which might be detracting from it.

Remember, it's okay to seek validation from others, *as long as your happiness and self-worth don't rely solely on it*. Healthy validation should be mutual and supportive. If you find yourself constantly chasing approval from someone who rarely gives it, or if they don't accept you for who you are, consider how this pursuit might be impacting your self-esteem.

Now that you've taken a closer look at the sources of external validation in your life, **it's time to shift your focus inward**. Understanding where you seek validation is important, but the journey to true confidence requires more than just recognising these patterns – it demands building a solid foundation of self-worth that isn't dependent on the opinions of others. This is where *my four essential truths* come in.

THE FOUR ESSENTIAL TRUTHS

These are four truths that have become the foundation for my own shift from external to internal validation. When I began to understand and apply them, they helped me break free from the cycle of constantly seeking approval and allowed me to step into, and express, my most authentic self.

1. No one is thinking about us as much as we think they are.
2. We never *really* know what other people think of us.
3. You can't please all of the people, all of the time.
4. It's not personal.

Let me explain each of these truths in more detail.

Truth 1: No one is thinking about us as much as we think they are

According to the renowned trauma expert Dr Gabor Maté, children naturally have an egocentric view of the world.[3] This means they think everything happening around them is directly related to them in some way.

I see this all the time with my son, Wolfe. If a dog walks near him, he will say, 'Mummy, look, the dog likes me!' But if a dog walks past him or in the other direction, he will ask, 'Why doesn't that dog like me?' The reality is that the dog's movements have absolutely nothing to do with him, but he is sure that they do. Maté explains that children, with their natural egocentric perspective, sometimes misinterpret events around them as being about them. For example, if parents argue or separate, a child might wonder if it's somehow their fault. However, with reassurance and clear communication, children can learn to understand that these events are not a reflection of their value or actions.

As we grow older, the lingering child-like part of our brain can continue to convince us that other people are thinking about us, even when there's no evidence to suggest they are. For example, you might feel self-conscious in the gym and be certain that everyone is looking at you and judging your technique. Or you might have a spot on your chin and assume that everyone you speak to is staring right at it, feeling repulsed by it. In psychology, this bias is known as the **spotlight effect**, which is when we assume that others are acutely aware of our perceived flaws.

But the simple truth is this: **most people aren't thinking about us as much as we think they are**. If you want proof of that, just ask yourself – how much time do you really spend thinking about other people? Do you analyse other people's technique in the gym? No, you focus on yourself and your own workout. If you were constantly looking around you, you'd get nothing done! Do you notice other people's spots when you're talking to them? No, and, even if you did, it would be a fleeting observation before refocusing on the conversation.

Remember, everyone is the main character in their own story. No one else is watching your show as intently as you are, and no one is desperately waiting for the next episode of your life to air. Honestly, most people just aren't as interested as you think they are. Instead of being paralysed by the fear of judgement, you can move through life with a renewed sense of freedom, knowing that others are just as absorbed in their own worlds as you are in yours.

> WHEN YOU REALISE THAT NO ONE ELSE IS CASTING A SPOTLIGHT ON YOUR FLAWS, YOU GAIN THE FREEDOM TO DANCE LIKE NOBODY'S WATCHING.

Truth 2: We never *really* know what other people think of us

We mentioned earlier that we tend to base our self-perception on our assumptions about what others think of us, rather than on their actual opinions. We pay attention to what people say, observe their body language and analyse their actions to draw conclusions about what they are thinking. However, we don't usually get it right. Our minds often distort reality, as we found out in Step 1 with thought filters (see page 30), and these misinterpretations can directly affect our confidence.

One of the cognitive distortions we discussed was 'personalising' – when we assume that a situation is directly related to us, without considering alternative explanations. For example, think about how often you've assumed a friend was upset with you because they didn't respond to your message right away. You might have spent hours or even days worrying about what you might have done wrong, only to receive a response later saying something like, 'I'm so sorry, I forgot to reply,' or 'I got distracted/busy and thought I had already responded.'

This tendency to personalise situations highlights the limitations of our ability to accurately gauge what others are thinking. We must remember that our interpretations are just that – *interpretations*, not facts. When we rely too heavily on our assumptions about others' thoughts, we can easily spiral into self-doubt and insecurity, all based on misunderstandings.

I learned this lesson first hand when I began hosting my in-person workshops. Having now delivered talks to rooms of all different shapes and sizes (ranging from small, to groups of ten, to huge rooms with thousands of people), I have noticed that when people watch you speak and they are concentrating, they often look intensely bored. I have to consciously remind my inner cheerleader to take over from my inner heckler so that my confidence doesn't crumble on stage. But I didn't know this when I delivered my first ever workshop, back in November 2019 . . .

As I spoke, I noticed a woman in the crowd wearing a pink tracksuit. Something about her facial expression made me absolutely certain that she hated me and thought the workshop was a complete waste of her money. After the interval, I couldn't believe she had returned to her seat. I was adamant she would leave because she was *clearly* having such an awful time. For the rest of the show, I couldn't shake the feeling that I was doing a terrible job and I began to feel increasingly self-conscious, which I am sure impacted my performance.

Then, two days later, I received an email:

> Hi Roxie,
>
> I came to your workshop on the weekend. I absolutely loved it and wondered if I could book in a one-to-one session with you.
>
> Maybe you'll remember me – I was wearing a pink tracksuit?

And that's when it hit me: **my inner critic is not to be trusted**, and I can't always rely on my own perceptions to gauge how others feel about me. My mind had taken ambiguous information (the woman's facial expression) and leapt to conclusions that reaffirmed my pre-existing insecurities and beliefs. My beliefs, emotions and past experiences had filled in the gaps with assumptions that simply weren't true.

Let that story serve as a reminder: **you never truly know what others are thinking; we are not mind readers and the stories we tell ourselves aren't always factually accurate.**

Truth 3: You can't please all of the people, all of the time

As we are talking about truths, I'm going to be very honest with you here: sometimes, when you think someone doesn't like you, *you're right*. Sometimes you aren't distorting reality with cognitive biases or distortions but you are, in fact, right on the money. But you know what? That is perfectly okay. **Because not being liked by everybody is inevitable, and the sooner we can accept that, the happier we will be.**

When I first started my career in self-development, my need to be liked triggered a cascade of doubts: 'Will people think I'm embarrassing? Cringey? Will they dismiss me as a joke, considering just a couple of years ago I was, by my own admission, a drug addict?' These thoughts were overwhelming at times, making me question whether I was even worthy of pursuing this path.

But then, I thought about all the people I really admired in the self-development space. I thought about people like Mel Robbins, Mo Gawdat, Brené Brown and Tony Robbins. I realised that, although there are so many people who love and respect them, there are also people who criticise or dislike them. That's when it clicked: if even the most respected and accomplished individuals face criticism, why should I expect to be any different?

Think about the people you love, admire and respect. Aren't there also people who dislike them? Of course! **No one in the world is universally liked** – not even Beyoncé, Taylor Swift or Dolly Parton. Probably not even David Attenborough (okay, maybe David Attenborough is an exception). But definitely not me and, I'm sorry, definitely not you either.

Understanding this felt like a weight was immediately lifted off my shoulders. I thought: 'Okay, some people are bound to not like me anyway. That's just how it goes. So, I may as well be myself and show up as authentically as I can.' I knew that by being authentic, and living in alignment with who I really am, I would attract the right people to me – those who understood me and liked me for who I was, not who I was trying to be.

> ONCE YOU LET GO OF THE NEED TO PLEASE EVERYONE (AN IMPOSSIBLE GOAL), YOU CAN FOCUS YOUR TIME AND ENERGY ON THE PEOPLE AND THINGS THAT REALLY MATTER TO YOU.

This shift in mindset has been invaluable to me and has also equipped me with the resilience to handle criticism, so that I don't allow it to shake my confidence. The other day, I was looking through my Instagram messages and I saw two that were sent just minutes apart.

One of them read, 'Roxie! I manifested with your book in January. I wrote about a dream job. I got a new job a month ago, and I just opened my notebook and was shocked to realise I'm now earning the exact salary I had written down. Thank you for writing such a life-changing book!'

The other one read, 'I bought your book and I have never read such drivel in my whole life. Would it be possible to ask for a refund?'

If I'd read those messages a few years ago, I would have fixated on the negative one and allowed it to feed my self-doubt. But instead, I was able to read them, fully appreciate the kind one and simply laugh off the other one. As my mum always told me, 'You can't please all the people, all the time.'

With the right mindset, you can read a negative comment without letting it impact how you feel about yourself. **Don't give power to those who want to put you down or dim your light.**

> **Note:** I'm not suggesting that you should completely disregard what others think of you. It's important to be mindful of how we interact with others and, of course, we should all aim to be kind, compassionate, considerate and respectful. Caring about the opinions of the people we love is natural and healthy. **Valuing our relationships and our interactions with the world helps us grow into better individuals.**
>
> However, the key is to recognise when our need for approval becomes excessive – when it's no longer helpful, when it starts to undermine our self-esteem and when it holds us back from realising our full potential.

Truth 4: It's not personal
'What someone thinks about you is none of your business.'

Growing up, how often were you told that the reason someone didn't like you was because they were jealous of you? As adults, we constantly try to reassure children that if someone doesn't like us, it doesn't mean there is something wrong with *us*. And yet, as grown-ups, we assume that when someone doesn't like us, it is *most definitely* because there is something wrong with us.

Despite the wisdom we try to impart onto children – reminding them that it's okay if not everyone wants to be their friend and encouraging them to not take others' opinions to heart – we often fail to apply the same advice to ourselves. When someone shows disinterest or disapproval towards us, instead of brushing it off, we internalise it, blame ourselves and immediately begin to question our worth, dissect our actions and search for flaws within ourselves.

The truth is, people's opinions are shaped by their own experiences, biases and often their own insecurities or struggles. **Their reactions to us say more about them than they do about us.**

But there's another layer to this that, in my view, makes it even easier to stop taking things so personally. **Everything in the world is made up of energy, and each of us operates on our own unique frequency.** I believe that this is why sometimes you'll encounter someone with whom you instantly click, and there's no logical explanation for it – it's just an effortless connection. And these connections don't always have to be deep or based on friendship, it's literally just an energy thing.

For example, there's a DHL driver who delivers parcels to my house once or twice a week. We've only ever exchanged a few words, but I genuinely enjoy seeing him – there's just a positive vibe between us. And at my local coffee shop, even though there are about ten different baristas I see a couple of days a week, there are two in particular I just really like and always share a nice exchange with. Can you think of someone like that in your life? Maybe it's the person you see often at the gym or the security at your office building. You might not know them well, but **there's something about their energy that feels good and makes you smile, even if you can't quite put your finger on why.**

And let's think about the friends you have. Is there one that you are completely different to in every way and, yet, something you can't describe bonds you and makes you feel like soulmates? *It's energy.*

On the other hand, there will inevitably be people who you simply do not connect with, no matter how hard you try. Perhaps there's a colleague who just rubs you up the wrong way; something about the energy between you feels off. Or maybe your best friend has been raving about her new friend she wants you to meet and, when you do, you can't quite grasp what she sees in them.

Just as there are people you'll naturally hit it off with, there will also be those with whom you don't share that same energetic alignment. **Some connections just aren't in sync, and that's okay.** It's not a reflection of your worth or theirs; see it simply as a matter of different frequencies. By accepting this, you can navigate social interactions with greater ease, letting go of the pressure to make every connection work. Instead, you can focus on nurturing the relationships that truly resonate with you and bring out the best in both you and them.

Let me offer one final analogy to emphasise this fourth truth: think of yourself as an inkblot. Bear with me here. In the 1920s, a psychological tool was developed called the 'Rorschach test'.[4] In this test, participants were shown an inkblot and asked to describe what they see. Although it's not widely used today, the test was designed to reveal aspects of a person's personality or complex mental states based on their interpretation of the inkblot. The key takeaway is that *everyone sees something different in an inkblot*. We could all look at the exact same image, yet each of us would interpret it differently, finding our own unique pictures and meanings. It's much like how we see shapes in clouds; one person might see a dragon, while another sees a rabbit.

People work the same way. Someone might look at you and see one thing, shaped by their own experiences and assumptions, while another person might see something entirely different. One person might find your honesty refreshing, while another might think you're blunt. Someone might think you're hilarious, while another person might think your humour is immature. If you try to change yourself to make everyone happy, you will lose who you really are. Remember: this isn't really about you — it's more about their individual interpretation of you. *You are the ink-blot.* So, don't take it so personally.

> ### FAQ
>
> Q: Someone doesn't like me, and I'm trying not to care, but it's really getting to me. What should I do?
>
> A: There will be occasions when someone puts you down, criticises you or makes it clear they don't like you – and it hurts. Sometimes it hurts because you admire that person, or some days it will simply hurt more than usual because your inner critic is already loud, you're tired or you're feeling vulnerable. Here's what I would do in those situations:
>
> **Normalise the experience**
> Remind yourself that everyone goes through this. Think back to the third truth: no one is liked by everyone.
>
> **Challenge the story in your mind**
> Often, when someone's negativity gets to us, it's because we start creating stories in our head – stories that we're not good enough, that we're fundamentally flawed or that this one opinion represents some larger truth. Catch yourself in the act of storytelling and ask, 'Is this true, or am I just reacting emotionally right now?' Think back to the Socratic questioning from Step 1: Master Your Thoughts (see page 35).
>
> **Shift your focus to gratitude**
> Reflect on the people who do love and appreciate you. You might find it helpful to write down their names or recall specific moments when they've supported you. Remind yourself that this one person's opinion is just that – one opinion – and it doesn't define who you are or how others see you.

Create a reset ritual
When someone's negativity triggers you, it's natural to feel stuck in the moment. That's where a personal reset ritual comes in – it's your tool for shifting your energy and clearing your mind. This could mean taking a walk to reconnect with nature, practising deep breathing to centre yourself or treating yourself to something small and comforting, like a cup of tea. Think of it as an intentional way to pause, refresh and reclaim your balance.

Set boundaries with your energy
Consider whether this person's opinion is even worth your attention. **Not everyone's perspective deserves space in your mind.** Visualise a protective bubble around yourself, one that keeps out unnecessary criticism and negativity. Think of it as reclaiming your energy for the things and people that actually uplift you.

Take pride in your authenticity
If someone doesn't like you, it may be a sign that you're stepping into your true self. That's a good thing! Authenticity isn't about pleasing everyone – it's about being aligned with who you are. Ask yourself: 'Would I rather be liked for pretending to be someone else or respected for being me?' Lean into your values and celebrate the fact that you're brave enough to be yourself.

Pro tip: Create a 'kindness bank'
Keep a folder (physical or digital) where you collect positive feedback and affirmations you've received. It might include thank you notes, compliments or messages from loved ones. When you're feeling low, revisit

> this 'kindness bank' to remind yourself of your value and the impact you've had on others. It's a tangible way to counterbalance negativity and reconnect with your worth.

STOP JUDGING OTHERS

One powerful way to reduce the influence of others' opinions is to stop judging others ourselves.

The reason this works is because of another of our cognitive biases: the **false consensus effect**. This bias leads us to overestimate how much other people share our thoughts, behaviours and 'norms'. In other words, we're wired to believe that others think like we do.

So, if we're in the habit of thinking or speaking negatively about others — like calling someone 'cringe' for posting something vulnerable online, or making rude comments about someone's lifestyle choices — we're more likely to believe that others are judging us just as harshly.

But here's the good news: by reframing how we perceive others with empathy and compassion, we can start to assume that others are doing the same for us. Whether or not they actually are is beside the point. This shift in our own behaviour can make us feel more positive about how others respond to us, and we can use the false consensus effect to work in our favour.

My dad once told me a story that taught me to do this from a young age:

There was a man waiting in line at the post office. Ahead of him was another man with two young children who were being rowdy and disruptive. The father seemed overwhelmed, visibly frustrated and impatient, while the children's behaviour drew tutting and judgemental glances from those around them.

The man in the queue decided to strike up a conversation with the father and soon learned that his wife had passed away just weeks earlier. The father was now trying to navigate life as a single dad to two grieving children. As others in the queue overheard the conversation, their attitudes shifted. The tutting stopped and, instead, people seemed to soften with understanding.

This story taught me two powerful lessons. First, that there is always more than meets the eye, and withholding judgement can prevent us from being unfairly critical of others. Second, it highlights that other people's behaviours are often a reflection of their own struggles, not a commentary on us.

So many people are fighting battles we can't see. Whether it's grief, stress or personal insecurities, everyone is dealing with their own challenges. The truth is, we rarely know the full story behind someone's behaviour. The next time someone behaves in a way that you don't agree with, instead of thinking, 'How rude,' try extending compassion towards whatever challenges they might be facing behind the scenes.

LETTING GO OF JUDGEMENT TOWARDS OTHERS CREATES SPACE FOR US TO BELIEVE THAT OTHERS ARE DOING THE SAME FOR US.

THE NEED TO BE LIKED AND DATING

Dating has a unique way of bringing our insecurities to the surface, often more powerfully than any other experience. The goal in dating is seemingly straightforward: to find someone we like and who likes us in return. But here's where many of us get stuck: we become so focused on being liked that we forget to consider whether we like the other person ourselves. We end up using dating as a tool for validation rather than a journey towards genuine connection. And when that validation doesn't come, our confidence takes a hit, fuelling the insecurities we already harbour about not being good enough.

I know this feeling all too well. I have left *countless* dates feeling crushed. Even, may I add, when I didn't like them and hadn't wanted to go on the date in the first place! Rather than thinking, 'We clearly weren't a good match, and that's okay,' I'd spiral into thoughts like, 'What's wrong with me? Why didn't they like me? Clearly I'm not pretty enough, cool enough or fun enough.' My need for approval was so overpowering that it clouded my ability to judge the situation rationally.

If you're currently dating and find it's chipping away at your confidence, I encourage you to flip your mindset before your next date. **Instead of saying, 'I hope they like me,' try saying, 'I hope I like them.'** This simple shift puts you in a more empowered position. It reminds you of your own value and what you bring to the table, rather than just worrying about how they might perceive you. When your mindset is centred around 'I hope they like me,' you're more likely to overlook red flags and pursue someone just to soothe your ego, rather than because they're actually a good match for you.

Since I made this mindset shift and understood the four truths I have just shared with you, my approach to dating is entirely different. Not too long ago, I went on a date with someone who was attractive and successful. We had great banter in our messages beforehand, so I was really excited and hopeful. But when we met, although we got along well, I quickly realised that our lifestyles and values didn't align. For instance, he had two tequila shots and two gin and tonics in the space of an hour, while I sipped on my Diet Coke. After the date, neither of us followed up with one another. In the past, I would've been hurt and felt rejected by the lack of contact, and probably reached out for a second date just to prove to myself that he would say yes. But this time, I felt completely at peace. We weren't right for each other, and that was okay. *It wasn't personal. Move on.*

I firmly believe that the universe has a way of steering us away from what isn't meant for us. It's not always as obvious as the experience I shared; sometimes we think we've found the perfect match, only to discover later down the line that they don't feel the same way. But that's when it's crucial to remember what you've learned in this step: **it's not about you**. It's likely more about where they are in their life or a mismatch in energy. The right person will see and appreciate you for *exactly* who you are – and they'll adore you for it.

> IT'S UP TO US TO LISTEN WHEN THE UNIVERSE NUDGES US, GUIDING US TOWARDS OR AWAY FROM SOMETHING. TRUST THE PROCESS AND KNOW THAT WHAT'S MEANT FOR YOU WILL FIND YOU.

LEARN TO SAY 'NO'

When we're so focused on being liked, we can end up making decisions that don't serve us – like saying yes to things that make us feel uncomfortable or compromising our values just to please others. Learning to say 'no' is one of the most empowering steps you can take to break free from the cycle of seeking approval.

In the past, I would have described myself as a people-pleaser. I would do anything to get people to like me, even if it meant giving away so much of my time and energy that I had nothing left for myself. A huge part of people-pleasing comes down to fear: the fear that people might stop liking or loving us unless we place their needs above our own.

This fear drives many of us to say yes to things we don't want to do, like going to a party when we're exhausted or agreeing to look after a friend's pet when we're already overwhelmed with responsibilities. Our deep desire to be liked can lead us to say yes when, deep down, we want to say no.

But here's the truth: we are deserving of love and respect just as we are – not because of what we do for others. Saying no is a way of reclaiming your time, energy and self-worth. It's about prioritising what truly matters to you, and trusting that those who care for you will understand and respect your boundaries.

When we struggle with low self-worth, it's easy to believe that our value lies in what we can give to others. But we have to remind ourselves that we are worthy of love simply because we exist. Saying no isn't about being selfish; it's about showing yourself the same care and consideration you extend to others.

If someone truly cares for you, they won't stop loving or respecting you just because you've set a boundary. And if they do? That's a reflection of them, not you.

✏️ EXERCISE: START SAYING NO

I know saying no can feel uncomfortable at first, especially if you're used to saying yes out of habit. But, just like building any muscle, the more you practise, the easier it becomes. Here are some steps to help you get started:

1. **Start small:** Begin with low-stakes situations. For example, decline a last-minute coffee catch-up if

your day is already full or say no to joining a group chat that doesn't interest you. These small wins will help build your confidence in setting boundaries.
2. **Use the 'no, but . . .' approach:** If you're struggling to say no outright, try offering an alternative that respects both your boundaries and the other person's needs. For instance:
   - If a friend frequently invites you out for drinks but it doesn't suit you, suggest brunch instead.
   - If someone asks to stay over during a hectic week, propose another time when you'll be able to enjoy their company more fully.

   This approach allows you to decline without feeling like you're letting anyone down.
3. **Remind yourself it's okay:** Most of the time, people won't care as much as you think they will. And they'll respect you even more for being honest and clear about your needs.

Saying no isn't just about setting boundaries – it's about recognising your own worth. It's a declaration to yourself that your time, energy and feelings matter.

As you get more comfortable saying no, you'll notice a powerful shift: you'll feel lighter and more in control of your life. You'll have more energy to say yes to the things that truly bring you joy and fulfilment.

FAQ

Q: But isn't saying 'no' just an excuse for being selfish and letting other people down?

A: This question comes up a lot, and I completely understand where it's coming from. Sometimes, saying yes – even when it's inconvenient – can be the right thing to do. To me, it all comes down to weighing up the cost and the benefit.

For example, let's say one of your close work friends invites you to her hen party, but you're worried that you won't know anyone. You might feel tempted to say 'no' because you don't want to feel left out. However, if this friend is important to you and attending the event would mean a lot to her, the benefit of going may outweigh the initial awkwardness. Plus, you might even find that you have a great time and make lasting friends and memories.

Another example might be a friend asking you to attend their small art show, even though you're tired. It might feel like an effort in the moment, but your presence could mean the world to them and give them the encouragement they need to continue their creative journey.

Showing up for the important moments in your loved ones' lives strengthens your bond, shows that you care and nurtures your relationships in a meaningful way.

That said, it's important to remember that saying no when something truly feels wrong for you isn't selfish – it's honest. It's about striking a balance: showing up for others when it counts while also protecting your own energy when you need to.

In the same vein, it helps to give others the same grace and respect we'd hope to receive in return. For example, if a friend cancels plans because they're overwhelmed or need to prioritise their mental health, can you avoid taking it personally? Could you respond with something

> like: 'Don't worry, I completely understand. Let's catch up when things settle down.'
>
> The more we practise this understanding with others, the more likely they are to offer us the same in return. We can all learn to get comfortable with others prioritising themselves, just as we're learning to prioritise ourselves.

FINAL WORDS

I hope you've begun to realise that the need to be liked, while deeply ingrained in us from childhood, doesn't have to control your life. The journey towards letting it go is not about shutting yourself off from others or disregarding their feelings; it's about understanding that **your worth isn't defined by anyone else's opinion**. It's about reclaiming your power and recognising that you have the ability to shape your self-worth from within.

We've explored how our desire for acceptance often leads us down paths of people-pleasing, fear of rejection and dependency on external validation. We've seen how these behaviours can erode our confidence, stifle our personal growth and disconnect us from our true selves. But we've also uncovered four truths that can help us break free from these patterns.

In the end, **the most important relationship you will ever have is the one with yourself**. So, make it a priority to build a strong foundation of self-worth that isn't dependent on external approval. As you do, you'll find that the freedom to be your authentic self is the most empowering gift you can give yourself.

STEP 4

BREAK FREE FROM
COMPARISON

Comparison is the thief of confidence.

ROXIE NAFOUSI — CONFIDENCE

It's widely understood that comparison is the thief of joy, but I also believe it's the thief of confidence. When we compare ourselves to others, we often measure ourselves against those we perceive as more successful, more attractive or more well-liked. In doing so, we trick ourselves into believing that we must be less worthy, less capable and less *enough* than they are.

Comparison shifts our focus away from what we have and all that we already are to what we lack and all the ways we feel that we fall short.

We compare ourselves to others in every area of our lives, but it's most intense where we feel the least secure. For example, if you struggle with self-doubt at work, you might find yourself constantly stacking up your professional achievements against your friends' and believing that those who earn more money or advance faster than you are simply better or more competent than you. Or imagine that you're single and desperately searching for a partner while your social media feed is flooded with engagement photos, wedding announcements and romantic getaways. The comparison might cause you to start asking yourself, 'What's wrong with me? Why haven't I found love when it seems that everyone else has? Am I not worthy of it?'

I get it – it can be really tough to watch others thrive in areas where you feel like you're falling behind. When I was struggling with addiction, seeing my friends on Instagram living healthy lifestyles was incredibly triggering. I envied their apparent self-control and the vitality they radiated in their photos, which felt like a painful contrast to my own reality.

When we start comparing our lives to others', we rob ourselves of our own joy, peace and growth. **Comparison can blind us from seeing all the abundance in our lives, and all that we have to offer the world and the people around us.**

To escape the comparison trap, we first need to understand where it comes from. There are two main reasons why comparison creeps into our minds so easily:

1. It's in our nature.
2. It's deeply ingrained in our culture and media.

COMPARISON IS IN OUR NATURE

On a subconscious level, we compare things all the time – whether it's lunch options at a café, nail colours at a salon or movies on Netflix. In fact, a 2008 study found that 12 per cent of all our thoughts are comparative, highlighting how deeply this instinct is woven into our thinking.[1]

Comparison does serve an important purpose: it helps us evaluate choices, guide our decisions, set priorities and make sense of our surroundings. For example, we weigh up the pros and cons when deciding whether to take a new job or stay with our current employer, and we compare prices when shopping to ensure we're getting the best deal. We even use comparison to gauge our physical well-being – checking how we feel today against how we felt yesterday to determine if we're getting sick or getting better after being unwell.

Beyond everyday choices, we also use comparison to understand ourselves. In 1954, the psychologist Leon Festinger developed what he called the 'Social Comparison Theory', explaining why we constantly measure ourselves against others.[2] According to his theory, we have an innate need to compare ourselves to others to determine our social standing, abilities and beliefs. When there's no objective information available, we rely on social comparison to understand where we fit in. **Comparison helps us make sense of the world, and where we belong in it.**

Just like the need to be liked, social comparison starts from a young age. When children are as young as three, they begin to notice their similarities and differences from others around them. They might notice things like, 'he's taller than me' or 'she has more toys'. As children grow older, these comparisons become more complex – they start noticing differences in skills, academic performance and social abilities, and begin measuring themselves against their classmates. It's at this stage that we start making what Festinger describes as 'downward' and 'upward' comparisons. Let me explain what these mean:

- **'Downward' social comparison:** This is when we compare ourselves to those we perceive as facing more challenges or struggling in ways we aren't. The goal of this type of comparison is often to boost our self-esteem, as it can help us feel grateful for our own situation.
- **'Upward' social comparison:** This involves comparing ourselves to those we perceive as better off, more successful or superior in some way. People who lack confidence often dwell on these comparisons, feeding their insecurities and feelings of inadequacy.

Studies have found that the lower your self-esteem, the more likely you are to make upward social comparisons.[3] **And the more you make upward comparisons, the lower your self-esteem becomes.** If you feel insecure about your skills, you will keep looking to highly skilled people to confirm that you are not as good as them. It's a vicious circle that keeps us feeling terrible about who we are and is another example of our confirmation bias at work.

COMPARISON IS DEEPLY INGRAINED IN CULTURE AND MEDIA

Think about what you watch, listen to and read – how often does it involve some form of competition or ranking? Sports leagues, talent shows, award ceremonies . . . they're all about figuring out who is 'the best'. Even in areas where outcomes are subjective, like movies or music, we often get caught up in identifying winners and losers. Our culture constantly pits people and things against each other, so it's no wonder that we end up doing the same in our own lives.

Today, the opportunities for comparison are practically limitless. In the past, you might have only compared yourself to people in your immediate circle – your family, friends, the local community or the celebrities you read about in magazines. When I was young, my main source of comparison, beyond the people I knew, were celebs on the front of *Smash Hits!* magazine. But now, social media has blown the doors wide open. We can compare ourselves to almost anyone, anywhere, anytime. Our feeds are filled with snapshots of other people's highlights, making it all too easy to fall into the trap of measuring our lives, and worth, against others.

Unsurprisingly, research has found that frequent social media use is linked to increased social comparison.[4] And a study from

2014 discovered that this social comparison led to decreased self-esteem and heightened anxiety.[5]

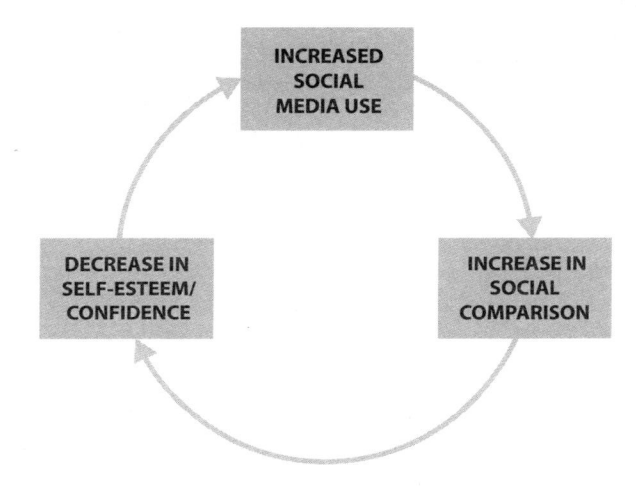

```
         INCREASED
          SOCIAL
         MEDIA USE
            ↑
   ↗                 ↘
DECREASE IN      INCREASE IN
SELF-ESTEEM/       SOCIAL
CONFIDENCE      COMPARISON
   ↖                 ↙
```

> **A note on social media:** I want to be clear that I don't believe social media is inherently bad. In fact, I personally love social media for many reasons – it helps me to connect to people all over the world and stay in touch with friends, and it has helped me build a platform from which I can share my mission and fulfil my purpose. But, like any relationship, it can turn toxic. Later in this chapter, we'll explore how to manage your social media habits to protect your confidence and well-being.

While comparison is a natural part of human nature and serves to help us understand, evaluate and navigate our world, it can become detrimental when it shifts from being a practical tool to a constant source of self-doubt and insecurity. **The challenge is not to eliminate comparison altogether, but to become**

aware of when it can help us and when it starts to hold us
back. Only by identifying the sources of our comparisons can
we begin to manage them in a healthier way.

To start this process, let's take a closer look at your personal
comparison triggers.

✏️ EXERCISE: UNDERSTAND YOUR COMPARISON TRIGGERS

Start by identifying who or what you're comparing yourself to,
and why.

Make a list

In the space on the next page, write a list of all the people or
situations that trigger feelings of comparison. Think about
anyone or anything that sparks emotions like envy, sadness,
resentment, bitterness or insecurity.

Also consider when these feelings crop up. Is it when you're with
certain friends, at work or scrolling through social media? Perhaps it's your sibling who always seems to make your parents/
caregivers proud, or a friend who's constantly posting about their
amazing holidays on Instagram. Write down how these situations
make you feel in as much detail as you can.

If nothing comes to mind right away, keep a diary over the next
week, noting down situations or people that make you feel envious or insecure.

....
....
....
....
....

Look for patterns
Pay attention to the patterns in your list. Are your comparisons mostly centred around relationships, career, money, appearance or popularity? Which insecurities do they tap into? Jot these down below.

....
....
....

Accept your feelings
The next step is to accept these feelings. I'm about to share some tools to help you stop these comparative thoughts from overwhelming you, but, for now, I invite you to simply accept that they exist. There's nothing wrong with feeling this way. A big part of what makes comparison so difficult is the shame that often comes with it – we don't want to compare ourselves to others, especially not people we know and love. But, as we've just explored, we live in a world that encourages us to do exactly that. We can't completely avoid comparison, so be compassionate and accepting of your feelings. Comparison is a natural human experience.

TOOLS TO COMBAT COMPARISON

Turn envy into inspiration

If you've read my first book, *MANIFEST: 7 Steps to Living Your Best Life*, you'll know that Step 6 in the manifestation journey is 'Turn Envy into Inspiration'. This step is all about shifting your perspective – transforming negative feelings into positive, helpful and motivating ones. It's such a powerful tool for dealing with comparison that I had to include it here, too.

Envy stems from a sense of lack, making us feel as though opportunities are limited. It often leads to a scarcity mindset, triggering feelings of fear and doubt. When we experience envy, we may think, 'They have something I want, and that means there's less available for me,' or 'They have something I want, and I will never be able to have it.' This mindset keeps us stuck, focusing on what we don't have instead of what we can achieve.

Inspiration is the antithesis of envy. Inspiration fuels an abundant mindset – it encourages us to think, 'If they can do it, so can I.' Rather than feeling threatened by others' success, we feel excited and motivated by it. We allow others to show us what is possible.

Think of envy and inspiration as two sides of the same coin. Envy drains our energy and sparks our self-doubt, while inspiration excites us and empowers us to take action. The good news is that, with awareness, we can take that envious feeling and *transform it* into inspiration. Here is how:

First, when you feel envy creeping in, be honest with yourself about it. Accept the feeling, and then **listen to it**. What is it telling you about your desires or areas that still need healing? Instead of letting envy overwhelm you, try to understand what it's showing you.

Next, knowing what desire it's pointing towards, **shift the thought to an inspired one**. For example, if a confident person walks into the room, instead of thinking, 'They're so bigheaded,' or allowing their confidence to make you feel small, try saying, 'Their confidence is so inspiring. I can't wait to walk into a room with that much confidence.' Essentially, instead of thinking, 'They have something I can't have,' say, 'They have something I want, and I know it's possible for me to have it too.'

I used to feel so inadequate when I was around successful and talented people. But now, I love being in those spaces because I see them as opportunities for growth. One of my favourite quotes is, 'If you're the smartest person in the room, you're in the wrong room.' Instead of feeling intimidated by those people, I see it as a chance to learn and evolve.

✎ EXERCISE: TRANSFORM ENVY INTO INSPIRATION

Over the next week, fill in the table below with any envious, comparative thoughts that come up. Then, replace them with a thought that makes you feel inspired.

I have started you off with a few examples:

Envy	Inspiration
'That person I went to university with already owns a successful business. I feel like a failure!'	'I would love to run a successful business. Perhaps I can learn from them to see what steps I can take to get my own project up and running.'
'My last remaining single friend is now in a relationship. Seeing how happy they are reminds me how unloveable I am.'	'It's exciting to realise how quickly things can change – this gives me hope that I will find love soon! I'll book some more dates to get the ball rolling.'

Return to this journaling exercise whenever you notice envy or comparison creeping in. Over time, with consistent practice, you'll find that your default reaction starts to shift. You'll naturally begin to see other people's achievements as motivation rather than a measure of your own shortcomings.

Keep reminding yourself that other people's success doesn't diminish your own potential.

THERE IS ROOM ENOUGH FOR US ALL TO SHINE.

Consider what you don't know

We know from Step 1: Master Your Thoughts that our brains rely on cognitive biases to fill in the gaps of our knowledge (see page 27). This happens all the time when we compare ourselves to others. For instance, you might assume that the girl you know on social media who just sold her business is living the life of her dreams, filled with constant joy, happiness and love. This assumption stems from what psychologists call the **illusion of knowledge**, where we mistake limited or surface-level information for the full picture.

But I think it's important for us to consider that every piece of information we have about someone else's life is just the tip of an iceberg. Beneath the surface lies an entire world you can't see – the struggles, insecurities and challenges they might be facing. Think about how many times you've been surprised by a friend's unexpected breakup or learned about a difficult part of someone's past that you never knew existed.

The truth is, everyone is dealing with something we don't know about. The more time I spend doing this work, the more acutely aware I become of this. I meet people all the time who confide in me about the battles they are facing and their hidden struggles – things that no one else would ever assume just by looking at them or their social media profiles. So, whenever you compare your life to an aspect of someone else's, ask yourself this simple question: **would I trade my *entire* life for theirs?**

Think carefully about what that trade would actually mean. You'd be taking on not just the parts of their life that you envy, but also the parts you don't see – their struggles, their setbacks and their pain. **Would you be willing to give up all the best parts of your own life, all the people and experiences that bring you joy, just for a snapshot of someone else's?** Likely not. Use this question as a grounding tool whenever you feel comparison creeping in.

Shift your perspective

When we're constantly making upward comparisons and looking up at people who we perceive to be ahead of us, we forget to see how far we have already come, and how many people might even be looking to us for inspiration.

Imagine being stuck in a traffic jam. Your focus is usually on the endless line of cars ahead, wishing you were further up, closer to the front. But what if you took a moment to glance in your rear-view mirror? You'd see all the cars behind you – drivers who joined the queue long after you did, likely wishing they were in your position. It's all about perspective.

Shifting your perspective doesn't mean looking down on others or seeing yourself as superior; it's about recognising that you have progressed so much further than you give yourself credit for. We are all on our own unique journeys, and wherever we are is perfectly okay. In fact, I would say that **wherever you are is exactly where you are supposed to be**.

Balancing upward comparison with a bit of downward comparison can provide a more grounded, realistic view of your life. It helps you see that you're not stuck at the bottom, but rather somewhere in the middle, doing just fine.

Remember: your normal day is someone else's dream.

Manage your relationship with social media

It's impossible to avoid comparison when we're constantly exposed to the highlights of others' lives on social media. The fundamental problem with social media comparison is that it's never a fair fight. **We're comparing our full, messy, complicated lives to the carefully curated highlights on someone else's feed.**

They say that a picture speaks a thousand words, but I would argue that a picture doesn't tell us nearly enough of the story. I've posted enough pictures on Instagram to tell you that behind every glamorous photo I've shared, there are hundreds that will never see the light of day. I've also seen this first hand at celebrity and influencer events, where people stage photos to present an idealised version of their lives. Once the cameras are away, the energy often fades and reality sets back in. It's not about deception; it's about the unspoken pressure to show up online, to look like we have it all together, even when we don't.

Even though many of us are aware of how heavily edited content can be nowadays, something that is becoming progressively worse with the introduction of AI, the impact of social media on how we see ourselves can be profound. Research shows that even knowing an image is manipulated doesn't always prevent its influence on how we perceive beauty, body standards or even the 'authenticity' of what we see.[6] And even when viewers are explicitly told that images of models in magazines or social media have been airbrushed or digitally altered, the idealised body image depicted still affects viewers' perceptions of beauty and self-esteem. This is because our brains often internalise the idealised images, even if we logically know they're unrealistic.

With all that being said, if social media has become a significant source of comparison or self-doubt here are some things you can do:

Consider taking a 'social media detox'
Social media detoxes are becoming increasingly popular and can provide a much-needed reset for your mental health. Even stepping away for a few days or weeks can help you gain perspective. And, if you find that life feels lighter without it, you might choose to take longer breaks or even delete your accounts altogether. The key is to find a balance that works for you and supports your well-being.

Limit how much you use it
If you feel like you *do* need to be on social media – or, at least, you don't want to lose the benefits of it – I invite you to rewrite the boundaries of your relationship with it. A 2019 study found that limiting social media use to 30 minutes per day significantly reduced feelings of loneliness and depression.[7]

Reduce the time you spend on social media to an amount that works around you and your life. You could consider setting specific times for checking social media – like during lunch, instead of first thing in the morning or right before bed. Turning off notifications can also help break the cycle of constant checking (I've done this and it has helped me immensely!).

Take control of your feed
You have more control over your social media feed than you might think. You don't *have* to follow celebrities who tap into your insecurities (seriously, unfollow them) and, thanks to the 'mute' button, you don't *have* to see constant updates from people who seem to just constantly remind you of what you lack. I mute people all the time, and it's not because I don't like that person or I'm being rude, I am just protecting myself from something that I know doesn't make me feel good. It doesn't

have to be forever, but it can help until you feel strong enough not to be triggered by comparison.

I often think about my friend who spent two years trying to conceive. She loved being on social media because it allowed her to connect with a community of women in a similar situation, which brought her a lot of comfort. However, it was also a double-edged sword. As she scrolled through her feed, she would often see pictures of pregnant women and babies – many of whom were her friends and family. Each time she saw them, she felt a pang of sadness.

I suggested she mute the accounts that triggered those feelings of sadness and comparison. At first, she felt guilty because she genuinely wanted to be happy for other women, especially her friends. But she recognised that she was in a vulnerable place, and protecting her mental health had to come first. The next time I saw her, she seemed lighter, no longer burdened by the constant reminders that had been weighing her down.

If you notice certain accounts are making you feel insecure or unhappy, pause and reflect. Is this content serving you or causing unnecessary stress? Ask yourself, 'Am I learning something valuable? Does this inspire me?' If the answer is no, consider muting, unfollowing or limiting your exposure. The goal is to create a feed that supports your well-being.

Practise gratitude
Gratitude is one of the most powerful antidotes to comparison. When we're caught up in comparing ourselves to others, it's easy to focus on what we lack rather than appreciating what we already have. Shifting our focus to gratitude can help us move from a mindset of scarcity to one of abundance.

Gratitude invites us to recognise and celebrate the good in our lives, counteracting the negativity that often accompanies comparison. It reminds us that we already have many blessings, even if they aren't always as visible or flashy as someone else's highlight reel.

Practising gratitude doesn't just make us feel better in the moment; it has the power to rewire our brains over time. Studies have shown that regularly practising gratitude can increase our overall happiness, strengthen our resilience and improve our relationships.[8] When we make gratitude a habit, we train our brains to more easily recognise the positive aspects of our lives, which naturally reduces the frequency and intensity of comparison.

Gratitude also helps us stay grounded in our own journey. We often compare ourselves to others who seem ahead of us, but gratitude helps us acknowledge our own progress and accomplishments. It creates a sense of contentment that allows us to appreciate where we are right now, rather than constantly yearning for what others have.

✏️ EXERCISE: START A DAILY GRATITUDE PRACTICE

To begin, set aside a few minutes each day to practise gratitude. You can do this in the morning to set a positive tone for the day or in the evening to reflect on the day's joyful moments.

In a notebook or journal, simply write down five things you're grateful for. These don't have to be big, monumental things; in fact, the smaller, more ordinary moments are often the most meaningful – maybe it's the first sip of your morning coffee, a text from a friend checking in or the satisfaction of completing a task you've been putting off. The key is to be specific and genuine in your reflections.

Gratitude is not just about listing what you have – it's about truly feeling appreciation for those moments, big or small. When you write them down, take a moment to savour each one. This helps you connect more deeply with the feeling of gratitude, making it so much more powerful and transformative.

When you catch yourself falling into the trap of comparison, take a deep breath and redirect your thoughts back to your gratitude practice. Reading over your journal entries can be a great way to remind yourself of the good in your life. The more you cultivate gratitude, the less power comparison will have over you.

FINAL WORDS

Comparison is a natural part of being human. It's something we all do, often without even realising it. For many of us, comparison – fuelled by social media – chips away at our confidence and sense of worth. But **it's time to shift your focus from what you lack to all that you already have**.

As you move forward, remember that escaping the comparison trap isn't about eliminating these thoughts altogether – it's about recognising them when they arise, understanding where they come from and choosing how you want to respond. Use the tools in this chapter to guide you: **turn envy into inspiration, consider what you don't know, shift your perspective, manage your relationship with social media and practise gratitude**. With every effort you make to shift your mindset, you're reclaiming your confidence, one thought at a time.

There's a quote I love: 'The grass is greener where you water it.' It's a powerful reminder that confidence grows when you nurture what you have, rather than wasting time and energy looking at what others appear to have. By investing in yourself and your own life, you create a sense of pride and fulfilment that no amount of comparison can shake.

Most importantly, remember this: there's only one person you should compare yourself to, and that's yourself. Compare who you are today to who you were yesterday and to who you want to become tomorrow. This kind of comparison isn't about tearing yourself down – it's about celebrating your progress, staying grounded in your own journey and embracing your growth.

Confidence isn't about being the best; it's about being committed to yourself, knowing your worth and trusting that you're exactly where you're meant to be.

STEP 5

CELEBRATE YOURSELF

Honour who you were, appreciate who you are and be proud of who you're becoming.

ROXIE NAFOUSI — CONFIDENCE

So far in the book, we have unravelled many of the biggest reasons we struggle with confidence: we engage in destructive thought patterns, we behave in a way that diminishes our self-worth, we're afraid of being judged or disliked and we compare ourselves to others. And most of this stems from one fundamental truth: we struggle with self-acceptance and self-love.

When we learn to accept ourselves fully – our strengths, our differences, our quirks and even our perceived flaws – we unlock the ability to **celebrate who we are**. Self-celebration isn't about believing we are perfect; it's about recognising our inherent worth, embracing our uniqueness and giving ourselves permission to shine.

I know that if you're struggling with low self-esteem, celebrating yourself can feel incredibly daunting. When you're so used to a critical inner dialogue, it may seem impossible to shift your focus to what's good. But remember, you are not just the main character in your story – you are also the writer. You have the power to change the script.

> WHEN WE CELEBRATE OURSELVES, WE ALLOW OURSELVES TO STEP INTO THE SPOTLIGHT THAT WAS ALWAYS RIGHTFULLY OURS TO CLAIM.

Many of us find it easy to celebrate other peoples' best qualities and achievements, yet find it incredibly hard to do the same for ourselves. My sister, Rana, is the perfect example of this. She is my biggest cheerleader, always showering me with compliments, encouragement and leaving sweet comments under every single one of my Instagram posts. Yet she is totally incapable of giving herself any kind of recognition.

Just last week, we were on a walk talking about her local netball team, which she has been playing for every Tuesday evening for the last couple of years. She mentioned that she organises the schedule, coordinates the team and even selects the players for each match.

'So, doesn't that make you the team captain?' I asked her.

'Not really . . .' she replied.

After pushing her a bit more, it became clear that she *was*, in fact, the team captain – but she didn't want to own that title because she was worried about appearing boastful. I laughed and said, 'What exactly do you think is going to happen? That I'm going to go home and say, "Wade, you won't believe how stuck up Rana has become; she called herself the team captain"?'

Maybe you can relate to this. Have you ever received incredible exam results but instead of admitting how hard you worked, you called it a 'fluke'? Or perhaps one of your ideas was chosen for a creative campaign at work, but you brushed off the credit, claiming it was a 'team effort'. Even when there's clear evidence of our achievements, many of us tend to downplay them.

UNDERSTANDING SELF-SERVING BIAS

Self-serving bias is a cognitive pattern where people tend to attribute their successes to internal factors, like their abilities or efforts, while blaming failures on external factors, such as bad luck or circumstances. In other words, most people naturally give themselves credit when things go well and shift the blame when things go wrong.

However, *for those with low self-esteem, this bias often works in reverse.* Instead of taking ownership of their successes, they downplay their role and give credit to external factors, like luck, help from others or good timing. This leads them to believe that their achievements were just a fluke, dismissing their hard work and talents.

It's important to challenge this reverse self-serving bias by actively recognising your contributions. Yes, external factors may have played a role, but your skills and efforts were at the heart of your success. This conscious recognition helps build a healthier relationship with your achievements.

WHY WE STRUGGLE TO SELF-CELEBRATE

There are a number of reasons why many of us struggle to celebrate ourselves. First, we live in a culture that heavily values humility and modesty. Secondly, and I think this is particularly prevalent for women, we are afraid of coming across as arrogant. And third, for some of us, there may be a deeper issue at play – feelings of shame that prevent us from fully accepting and celebrating who we are.

Let's explore these reasons a little further . . .

We glorify humility

> HUMILITY (noun): *The quality of having a modest or low view of one's importance.* (*Oxford Languages*)

Humility has been regarded as a desirable character trait across cultures for centuries. Both the Bible and the Quran teach that humility is an important characteristic for good faith and character. It's also a cornerstone of Hinduism, reflected in the practice of yoga, and Buddhism, where it is linked to selflessness and the reduction of ego. Philosophers like Aristotle and Socrates also highlighted the necessity for humility when it comes to acquiring knowledge – because, in order to learn, you first have to recognise your own limitations.

There's a reason why humility has been so valued across cultures, faiths and generations: it keeps us grounded. It helps us stay balanced, enables us to give back to the world and allows for personal growth.

Humility *is* a valuable trait. The problem arises when it's pushed too far. The need to be humble has become so ingrained in many of us that it often drives us to put ourselves down and magnify our flaws. From a young age, we're taught not to boast or 'show off'. We're repeatedly told, 'Don't talk too much about yourself,' or 'It's not polite to brag.' While these messages were likely well-intentioned, they can leave a lasting impact. We grow up associating self-celebration with arrogance, and we feel guilty acknowledging our successes.

This belief was heavily reinforced in my own life through cultural practices. Growing up, my mum often warned me about the 'evil eye'. In Middle Eastern culture, there's a strong belief that showing off or celebrating yourself too openly invites jealousy and bad energy. I remember when I moved into my first flat, my mum insisted I leave a dirty shoe in the hallway – a tradition meant to prevent people from becoming envious of your home. Her fear, that she passed on to me, was that if we attracted the evil eye, we would experience harm or bad luck. While the intention behind these practices is rooted in protection, they also taught me to hide my joy, minimise my achievements and fear being too visible. Even now, I still have a lingering fear that when I post an achievement on Instagram or simply appear happy, I will attract negative attention and criticism as a result. This fear of being too visible, of having my happiness targeted, is something I continue to work through.

Whether through cultural beliefs or everyday sayings, many of us carry the weight of humility to the point that we become afraid to celebrate ourselves. But here's the truth: when taken too far, **humility can prevent us from recognising our own value**. We shy away from deserved praise and shrink ourselves to avoid standing out.

There's a big difference between being humble – recognising that we are not better than anyone else, and that we still have so much to learn – and diminishing our worth entirely.

Humility is often linked to how we accept praise, and our response to compliments can reveal a lot about our relationship with it. In an effort to be humble, we often end up dismissing or downplaying them. I have a friend who does this all the time. The other day, she posted an incredible, elaborate three-tier cake she made for her daughter's birthday party. I messaged her to say how amazing it looked and how impressed I was. She replied, 'Oh, it was much easier than it looked, I just followed a recipe I found online. And honestly, it didn't taste that good.' Despite clearly putting effort and skill into it, she couldn't allow herself to own the praise.

True humility isn't about rejecting compliments or dimming your light. It's about being able to graciously accept acknowledgement without feeling the need to deflect. A simple 'Thank you, I really appreciate that,' allows you to accept recognition while staying grounded. This kind of response reflects ***healthy humility*: recognising your value without overstating or shrinking from it.**

> **Challenge:** The next time you receive a compliment, resist the urge to explain it away. Instead, practise simply responding with those two magical words: 'thank you'. Then, if it feels natural, offer a kind word in return. This exchange creates an opportunity for both you and the other person to feel good.

Humility, when balanced, allows us to grow and stay grounded without overshadowing our self-worth.

IT'S CRUCIAL TO RECOGNISE OUR
ACHIEVEMENTS WITHOUT FEAR.

We fear coming across as arrogant

ARROGANT (adjective): *Having or revealing an exaggerated sense of one's own importance or abilities.* (*Oxford Languages*)

Just as humility is celebrated in many cultures and faiths, arrogance is often viewed as one of the least desirable traits. I'm sure we can all think of someone who we would describe as arrogant. Maybe you have a colleague who always talks over you and thinks their ideas are better than everyone else's. Or perhaps you have an acquaintance who constantly boasts about all the fun parties they go to, what celebrities they've met and how much money they have, while never taking the time to ask you questions about your life.

It can be frustrating to engage with people like this. Their behaviour tends to create an environment where it's easy to feel overlooked and their presence can make others feel small or intensify feelings of self-doubt. So, it's unsurprising that many of us, especially those who are sensitive to how they're perceived, try hard to avoid being seen this way. For women, especially, this can be even more pronounced, as we're often conditioned to be modest and to avoid drawing attention to ourselves.

The challenge is that in trying to steer clear of arrogance, we can end up swinging too far in the opposite direction. We tell ourselves that *any* display of self-belief might be seen as boastful, so we end up not celebrating ourselves at all.

But here's the thing: **you can celebrate yourself, and be confident, without being arrogant.** They are not the same thing. Confidence isn't about thinking you're better than anyone else – it's about trusting your abilities and being comfortable in your own skin.

To help clarify the difference between arrogance and confidence, let's break it down:

Arrogance	Confidence
Overestimation of abilities: Arrogant people tend to have an inflated sense of their abilities and achievements. This means they think they are superior to others, and they dismiss other people's suggestions and contributions.	**Self-assurance:** You trust your skills and judgements. It doesn't mean you think you're superior to anyone else; it just means you respect yourself, and you have faith in your abilities.
Disrespect for others: In believing that they are 'the best', arrogant people might belittle or demean those they see as inferior.	**Respect for others:** You acknowledge and respect other people's contributions. You don't feel threatened by other people's abilities, and you can collaborate effectively to utilise everyone's skills.
Rejection of feedback: Since they inflate their own abilities, arrogant people tend to be resistant to feedback, viewing it as a threat rather than an opportunity. They may become defensive or dismissive when they're challenged.	**Openness to feedback:** You are able to view constructive criticism and feedback as an opportunity to grow and improve.
Distorted self-perception: Arrogant people tend to ignore or deny their weaknesses.	**Realistic self-perception:** You understand your strengths – but also your weaknesses. You can recognise your limitations, and ask for help when needed.

Negative influence on others:	Positive influence on others:
Arrogant people are usually very difficult to be around, creating a toxic environment for everyone in their orbit.	Expressing your positive traits and talents helps to motivate and inspire people – because when you're confident, it gives other people confidence too.

Arrogance says: 'I'm the best.'
Confidence says: 'I'm working towards the best version of myself that I can be.'

It's important to understand that confidence and arrogance are often mistaken for one another, but they couldn't be more different. Arrogance is often a facade, a way to mask insecurity by inflating one's sense of importance, often at the expense of others. On the other hand, confidence comes from a place of inner assurance. It doesn't rely on external validation or require others to be 'less than' in order for you to feel 'more'.

Where arrogance seeks to dominate, true confidence seeks to connect. When you're confident, you know your value, but you don't feel the need to broadcast it to everyone. You trust your abilities, but you also recognise that other people have their strengths too. You're comfortable sharing space, listening to others and giving credit where it's due because you don't feel threatened by the success or talents of those around you.

TRUE CONFIDENCE DOESN'T SHOUT;
IT'S FELT IN QUIET STRENGTH.

So remember: **you can be humble and confident at the same time**. It's possible to recognise your worth, celebrate your achievements and still remain grounded. Confidence is about embracing your strengths while also respecting the strengths of others.

P.S. If you're worried about coming across as arrogant, you're likely on the right track. Arrogant people often lack the self-awareness to even realise it.

We carry shame

> SHAME (noun): *A painful feeling of humiliation or distress caused by [the belief in being] wrong or foolish.* (*Oxford Languages*)

Shame can be an invisible weight many of us carry, often tied to parts of our identity we feel we need to hide or downplay. Whether it's because of our background, experiences or something deeply personal, shame keeps us from fully embracing, and celebrating, who we truly are.

Growing up, I carried a deep shame about who I was. In the midst of the Iraqi war, I knew that Iraqis were considered the 'enemy' and Islamophobia was rife. When I was 11 years old, a group of girls locked me in a phone box and chanted 'Saddam' outside – a cruel reference to the Iraqi dictator, Saddam Hussein. That incident pushed me to change schools, but it also led me to try to reinvent myself in a way that I thought would protect me. I began telling people I was from Jordan instead of Iraq, and I changed my name from Rawan to Roxie. At the time, I thought I was shielding myself from judgement, but in reality, I was rejecting who I was and the shame I carried was slowly eroding my self-worth.

I know I'm not alone in this experience. Many people hide aspects of themselves out of fear of rejection. I've had countless conversations with people who've done the same. One of my good friends, for example, hid his sexuality from his parents until his thirties, terrified they would disown him. For years, he avoided certain conversations and changed the way he talked about his life to avoid being honest about who he truly was. It was only when he opened up that he began to feel a profound sense of relief and freedom. The weight of shame that he had carried for so many years started to lift, and he was finally able to live his life authentically.

A client of mine, a successful CEO, experienced something similar, but in a different context. She came from a working-class background and worked incredibly hard to rise through the corporate world. But once she reached a certain level of success, she felt immense pressure to hide her roots. She even went so far as to change her voice, adopting what she felt was a more 'professional and respectful' accent to avoid any hint of her upbringing. It wasn't until we worked together that she began to realise how much energy she was wasting on hiding an important part of who she was. Over time, she started speaking more freely, with pride in the journey that had brought her to where she was.

So many of us can relate to a version of this story; we hide parts of ourselves that we've been taught to believe are 'less than' or 'not good enough'. But the truth is, **these are often the very parts that make us unique and give depth to who we are.**

Ultimately, we have to recognise that the shame we feel is because we fear other people's prejudice, bias and ignorance. The fear of rejection often exaggerates the potential outcomes, but, more often than not, people surprise us with their acceptance and compassion. And even if we do face rejection, it says more about the other person's limitations than our own worth.

The moment I started telling people I was Iraqi, I felt an enormous sense of relief. I came to accept that some people might still stereotype or judge me, but that was their problem, not mine. Being honest about my identity seemed to lift the weight of shame, but even more than that, it transformed it into pride. What once made me feel embarrassed is now a part of me that

I cherish. I stopped running from my roots, and instead began to embrace my culture and my heritage. In doing so, my self-worth began to heal and grow.

IF WE CAN TRANSFORM SHAME INTO ACCEPTANCE, THEN WE HAVE A FOUNDATION FROM WHICH TO BUILD SELF-LOVE.

✏️ EXERCISE: SHAME JOURNAL

I invite you to consider if and how shame plays a role in how you view yourself, using the prompts below.

- What parts of myself do I hide from the world?
  ....
  ....

- How does the thought of revealing these parts make me feel?
  ....
  ....

- How does keeping them hidden affect me?
  ....
  ....

- Does holding on to this shame serve me, or is it holding me back?
  ....
  ....

- How might it feel to be fully open about these parts of myself?
  ....
  ....

Overcoming shame is a journey, and it often starts with small steps towards honesty and vulnerability. Here are a few ways to begin:

- **Open up to someone you trust:** Sharing your story with someone close to you can help alleviate the burden of hiding. Often, this first step opens up space for deeper acceptance.
- **Join a community:** Whether it's a support group, an online space or a hobby group, finding people with similar experiences can help you feel understood and less isolated.
- **Practise self-compassion:** Gently remind yourself that everyone has parts of their identity they struggle with. Start small, acknowledging those parts of you without judgement, and affirm that they deserve to exist just as much as any other.

Take a moment to acknowledge the courage it takes to confront those hidden parts of yourself. Remember, the journey to self-acceptance is about embracing every part of yourself, even the ones you've kept in the shadows. As you begin to let go of that shame, you create more space for self-compassion, authenticity and, ultimately, self-celebration.

We've uncovered some of the key obstacles that hold us back from truly celebrating ourselves: taking humility too far, fearing that we'll come across as arrogant and a lingering sense of shame that keeps us from embracing our true selves. With this understanding, it's time to challenge these limiting beliefs and start embracing self-celebration.

In my view, self-celebration rests on two main pillars:

1. Taking pride in your strengths.
2. Embracing your authenticity.

Within each of these areas, I've provided practical tools to help guide you on your journey to self-love and confidence.

TAKE PRIDE IN YOUR STRENGTHS

Self-awareness has already come up several times throughout these steps because it's a crucial springboard for change. So far, we've focused on some of the more challenging aspects of self-awareness, like recognising our triggers, bad habits and unhelpful patterns. But now, it is time to shift our awareness onto something more uplifting: *recognising and celebrating all the incredible qualities that make you, you*.

You might be thinking: 'I don't know what I'm good at or what I can celebrate about myself.' But I want you to trust me on this: **every single person has strengths, talents and unique characteristics that are worthy of pride and celebration.** Sometimes, you just need a little help to see them clearly.

There's actually a cognitive bias that explains why so many of us struggle to recognise our own strengths and abilities – and it's called the 'Dunning-Kruger Effect'. Coined by psychologists David Dunning and Justin Kruger in 1999, this bias highlights how people who are less skilled at something tend to overestimate their abilities because they aren't fully aware of what they don't know.[1] Conversely, those with more expertise often downplay their skills because they better understand the complexities involved. **In other words, novices can be overconfident, while experts can be underconfident.**

A simple example of this came up during a conversation with a colleague of mine who has always been an incredible listener. She has this unique way of making people feel deeply seen and heard, offering insights and advice that always feels thoughtful and considered. But when I pointed out how special her ability to do this was, she brushed it off, saying, 'It's not a big deal. I just listen. Everyone can do that.' *But not everyone can.* Her empathy and communication skills were something that came so effortlessly to her that she couldn't see them for the rare and valuable qualities they truly were.

RECOGNISING YOUR UNIQUE GIFTS IS THE FIRST STEP TO FULLY EMBRACING AND CELEBRATING THEM.

I want to help you fast-track the process of recognising all the things that make you wonderfully unique. By noticing and celebrating your strengths, you'll build trust in your own abilities and start seeing just how much you have to offer the world and those around you.

Uncover your virtues and strengths

To begin identifying where your strengths lie, it helps to explore the core traits that shape your character.

One great framework is the **six virtues of positive psychology**, developed by psychologists Christopher Peterson and Martin Seligman in their research on character strengths.[2] These six virtues represent core characteristics that are universally valued across cultures and play a significant role in positive mental health and personal development.

Each 'virtue' includes multiple corresponding character strengths (24 in total). Understanding and embracing these strengths can give you insight into what makes you special and where you naturally shine.

Take a moment to go through the table below and think about which qualities resonate with you. This is your opportunity to recognise the positive traits that may have been overlooked or undervalued in yourself.

The Six Virtues	Associated Character Strengths
Wisdom and Knowledge: These strengths help us acquire and use information effectively, allowing us to make good decisions, offer advice and solve problems.	**Creativity:** Thinking of novel and productive ways to do things (it's not always limited to being artistic). **Curiosity:** Taking an interest in things, finding subjects and topics fascinating, exploring and discovering. **Open-mindedness:** Thinking things through and examining information from all sides, weighing up information in a balanced way. **Love of learning:** Mastering new skills and topics. **Perspective:** Having ways of looking at the world that make sense to other people, being able to offer good advice.
Courage: These strengths allow us to achieve goals in the face of opposition, fostering resilience and determination.	**Bravery:** Speaking up for what is right (even if it's unpopular), not shying away from difficulty, challenges or pain.

Perseverance: Finishing what you start, keeping going even when things get difficult and taking pleasure in completing tasks.

Honesty: Speaking the truth, acting authentically and taking accountability for your own feelings and actions.

Zest: Approaching life with excitement, energy and enthusiasm. You throw yourself into things and don't do them half-heartedly.

Humanity: These strengths help us to foster meaningful relationships and enhance positive social interactions.	**Love:** Valuing close relationships with others, being close to people – whether romantically or platonically.

Compassion: Doing good deeds for others, helping them and taking care of them.

Emotional intelligence: Having empathy and being aware of other people's feelings and motives. You understand how to adapt to social situations.

Justice: These strengths allow us to build trust in communities and groups.	**Teamwork:** Working well as a member of a team, being loyal to a group and doing your share.
	Fairness: Treating all people with equality and respect, without letting your personal feelings bias your decisions about others.
	Leadership: Encouraging a group to get things done while maintaining good relationships with all involved. You organise group activities and ensure that they happen.
Temperance: These strengths help us to regulate behaviours and emotions, preventing harm to ourselves and others.	**Forgiveness:** Giving people a second chance, not being vengeful and believing that everyone has the capacity for change.
	Humility: Letting your accomplishments speak for themselves and not regarding yourself as any more important than anyone else.
	Prudence: Being careful about your choices, not saying and doing things that you might later regret.

	Self-control: Regulating what you say and do, being disciplined and staying in control of acting on your appetites and emotions.
Transcendence: These strengths encourage a sense of purpose, allowing us to connect to the world in a meaningful way.	**Awe:** Noticing and appreciating beauty and excellence in all areas of life, from art and science to any everyday experience. You appreciate all that life has to offer.
	Gratitude: Being aware and thankful for good things that happen.
	Hope: Having optimism about the future and working on achieving it.
	Humour: Liking to laugh and/or make other people laugh. You are able to see the lighter side of life.
	Spirituality: Believing in a higher purpose – not necessarily in terms of religion. You have beliefs about the meaning of life that provide comfort and shape how you conduct yourself.

✏️ EXERCISE: RECOGNISE YOUR CHARACTER STRENGTHS

Identify your strengths

Carefully review the table and then pick out the associated character strengths that resonate with you the most. There's no right or wrong number, but I encourage you to choose at least five that feel true to who you are.

> **Note:** If you're struggling with this, don't hesitate to ask for help from your loved ones. Ask someone you trust to go through the table with you and highlight the strengths they see in you. You might be surprised at what they say! It's often easier for others to recognise positive qualities in us than we can see in ourselves. Why? Because we're privy to all our internal doubts, fears and insecurities, making it harder to see ourselves as clearly.

Write down examples

Let's take it a step further. It's time to bring your strengths to life by using the space on the next page to write down real-life examples that demonstrate these qualities in action. Think back to moments when these strengths naturally shone through – no matter how big or small. The goal here is to reinforce your sense of self-awareness and pride in what you've already accomplished.

Here are a few examples to guide you:
- **Creativity:** I designed my own invitations for my wedding and people still compliment me on how unique they were.
- **Perspective:** A friend was feeling overwhelmed about a big decision and I helped them weigh up the pros and cons by breaking things down and offering a

balanced view. They told me afterwards that it helped them feel clearer and more confident in their choice.
- **Compassion:** I always make time to check in on my friends when I know they're going through a tough time, even if it's just sending a quick text to let them know I'm thinking of them.

....
....
....
....
....
....

Reflect on your strengths

As you review your list, notice if there's any overlap among your strengths. Do they tend to cluster around a certain virtue, like 'Courage' or 'Humanity'? Embrace these qualities and feel genuinely proud of them. These are the building blocks of your unique self – let that good feeling sink in.

> **Note:** If you want to explore your strengths further, below are two great resources to help you:
>
> 1. **The 16 Personalities Test:** This can help you work out what kind of person you are – from 'The Mediator' to 'The Entrepreneur' to 'The Entertainer'. Take the test on 16personalities.com.
> 2. **The Cambridge Code:** Created by Dr Emma Loveridge and Dr Curly Moloney, this insightful test delves into your subconscious brain and provides deeper self-understanding. Learn more at thecambridgecode.com.

Rediscover your everyday skills

When you think about your skills, what comes to mind? Chances are, you think of the types of things you'd list on your CV – skills that seem valuable in the workplace or that you feel might 'impress' others. But the truth is, some of the most impactful skills in our lives are the ones that don't often get recognised because they feel somewhat unremarkable. Yet these everyday skills are the ones that make the biggest difference in how we live, love and support those around us.

For example, your ability to diffuse a tense situation with humour, remember the little details that make someone feel seen and valued, or adapt quickly when plans fall through – these are not just 'small' things; they are the core of how you connect with others and manage the world around you. These everyday acts are proof of your strength, resilience and capacity to care. And even though they might not be celebrated in the same way as professional achievements, they are essential to your life and relationships.

Some examples of everyday skills include:

- **Organising a chaotic day:** Whether it's managing a packed schedule or juggling multiple demands, you find a way to make it all work smoothly.
- **Keeping things running:** Managing household tasks or logistics, like making sure bills are paid or that everyone gets where they need to be in time.
- **Welcoming others:** Making everyone feel included at a gathering, ensuring no one feels left out or overlooked.
- **Being the prepared one:** Always having just what's needed – an extra tissue, a plaster or a snack – making others feel cared for in small but meaningful ways.

✏️ EXERCISE: IDENTIFY YOUR EVERYDAY SKILLS

I invite you now to take a moment to reflect on the skills you've been overlooking.

1. **List your everyday skills:** In the space below, reflect on the ways you support those around you, manage your day-to-day life and cope with responsibilities. Think about both the big and small acts that help you and those around you thrive.
2. **Acknowledge their worth:** Take time to consider the positive impact these skills have. How do they make things easier, more joyful or more connected? Write down the ways they add value to your relationships, household or community. Appreciate their importance and the role they play in shaping your well-being and the well-being of others.

....
....
....
....
....
....
....
....
....
....

Embracing and celebrating these everyday skills is a powerful act of self-celebration. When you acknowledge these strengths, you recognise the many ways you show up for others and for yourself, reinforcing your own sense of worth. It's easy to overlook the things you do out of habit or care, but these skills are essential to the fabric of your life; they are the glue that holds so many aspects of life together. Give them the recognition they deserve.

Celebrate how far you have come

Let's pause for a moment and reflect on your journey so far. Often, we get so caught up in chasing what's next that we forget to acknowledge just how much we've already achieved. There's a quote I love: 'Remember the time we wished for the things we have now.' It's such a simple but powerful reminder that many of the milestones we've reached today were once our deepest hopes and dreams. Whether it's the career you've built, the relationships you've nurtured or the many ways you've grown, matured and evolved, they all deserve to be acknowledged and celebrated.

I want to give you an opportunity to think about all the choices, effort, consistency and resilience that it took to get to where you are today. These are not things to be taken lightly. Celebrating your own journey not only allows you to feel proud of yourself, but also helps you to build confidence in what you can accomplish moving forward.

✏️ EXERCISE: CELEBRATE YOUR ACHIEVEMENTS

This is one of my favourite exercises, and one that I really hope you will allow yourself to indulge in.

Take out your notebook or journal, or a large piece of paper, and give yourself time to reflect on the following questions:
1. **What are some meaningful achievements you're proud of?** *Consider reflecting on achievements from the past year, but feel free to go further back if something stands out.* These can come from any area of your life, whether it's your career, your relationships or your

personal growth. I encourage you to dive into the details, no matter how big or small. Remember, this is all about self-celebration.
2. **What internal qualities helped you along the way?** Think back to the strengths you identified in the earlier exercise (page 142). Did some of those, such as resilience, creativity, determination or compassion, play a role? Recognise your strengths and celebrate how they helped shape your journey.
3. **What challenges did you have to overcome to reach that point?** Reflect on the obstacles you faced and how you navigated through them. Acknowledge the effort it took to overcome these challenges.
4. **How do these achievements make you feel today?** As you reflect on what you've accomplished, allow yourself to feel the pride, joy or satisfaction that comes with acknowledging your journey. Write down these emotions and let them sink in.

Every accomplishment, big or small, is a testament to your unique strengths, and you ought to give yourself the credit you deserve. Celebrating your achievements is more than just a momentary pat on the back – it's a powerful way to honour your journey and reinforce your sense of self-worth.

Moving forward, please remember to pause and appreciate your journey, not just when you reach a destination, but at every step along the way. You are worth celebrating, and every milestone, no matter how seemingly small, is evidence of your growth.

> **Note:** Something I love to celebrate are those moments when I realise I've handled a situation differently to how I would have in the past. For example, last weekend I found myself in a conversation where I was informed that a friend of mine had been gossiping about me behind my back, telling and exaggerating private details that I had shared with her. In the past, I would have got upset, felt hurt and immediately gone to the girl to confront her – which would have inevitably created further drama and upset. Instead, I did nothing. I didn't allow it to hurt me or impact how I felt; I just took is as a lesson learned and moved on as gracefully as I could. To me, that reaction served as proof of my growth, and I felt immensely proud of that.
>
> I encourage you to take note of the times when you behave, respond and act differently to how you might have in the past. Acknowledge and celebrate not just how far you have come, but how much you have grown.

EMBRACE YOUR AUTHENTICITY

In Step 3: Stop Trying to Be Liked by Everybody, we explored the need to be liked and discussed that while it is natural to want to fit in, this desire can often lead us to alter parts of ourselves to mould into what we believe is 'normal' or desirable. **In trying to conform, we dampen our individuality and the unique traits that make us who we are.** Much of this can stem from a sense of shame – which we explored earlier in this chapter (page 132). Whether it's about our background, our passions or our quirks, this shame can drive us to hide parts of ourselves out of fear of rejection. Essentially, it holds us back from being authentic.

Authenticity – the quality of being 'real' or true – is a non-negotiable piece of the confidence puzzle. Studies show that people who report higher levels of authenticity also report higher levels of self-esteem.[3] Research has also shown that **the more you act in alignment with your authentic self, the more confident you feel**.[4]

However, when we suppress our authentic selves, we often experience **cognitive dissonance**. This typically occurs when our actions conflict with our true beliefs, values or desires, leading to mental discomfort. Think about a time when you felt like you had to put on a mask to fit in – maybe at work, with friends or even with family. How did you feel? Uncomfortable? Well, that uncomfortable, 'off' feeling is cognitive dissonance at play. It's your mind's way of telling you that there's a gap between how you're acting and who you really are.

I used to experience this a lot with a certain group of friends that I was desperate to fit in with. The men were all wildly successful, cool and well dressed, and the women were all supermodels and actresses who had effortless charisma. Whenever I'd get invited to one of their parties, I'd feel so excited and honoured, thinking that if I was part of the 'cool' group, it might make me feel better about myself as a result. But whenever I was with them, I'd always feel so uncomfortable and nervous. I'd walk in and just shrink. They would be talking about things I couldn't relate to, like the private jet they went on or their month-long holiday in St Tropez. Don't get me wrong, I was genuinely happy for them and loved listening to the fabulous stories that were like something out of a movie, but I felt like I had to pretend I was someone I wasn't to make conversation. I didn't feel they'd be too interested in me talking about Wolfe or what I cooked for dinner last night or the fact I went to bed before 9pm every night that week.

Then one day, the penny dropped: why was I putting myself in these situations? I didn't need the 'cool kids' to make me feel worthy or loveable. Instead, I decided to spend more time with people who made me feel at home – friends with whom I could be utterly and entirely myself. The last time I got invited to one of those parties, I said no, and it felt so damn good. *Goodbye cognitive dissonance; hello authenticity.*

Living in alignment with our true selves isn't just about pursuing what we love – it's about recognising and embracing the parts of us that make us feel whole. When we suppress those parts, we risk living with a constant feeling that something isn't right. But when we honour who we truly are, we reduce cognitive dissonance, unlocking a sense of ease and magnetic confidence.

I had a client who always loved to dance. As a child, she would spend hours practising in her room, completely lost in the joy of movement. But, as she grew older, she felt pressured to put her passions aside in favour of a more 'practical' career path that her family and community would respect.

By her early thirties, she had built a successful career, but she still felt dissatisfied and unfulfilled. During one of our sessions, I asked her about a moment when she felt truly happy. Without hesitation, she described the freedom and joy of dancing – of moving her body freely, of expressing emotions that couldn't be put into words. That was when it became clear: she had abandoned a part of herself that made her feel alive.

I encouraged her to reconnect with dance – not as a career change, but as a way to reclaim that lost piece of identity. She joined a dance class at her gym and, although at first she felt a little awkward, the joy and freedom she once knew quickly returned. This small act of self-expression rippled through her life: she showed up at work more confidently, felt more connected in her relationships and exuded an energy that others couldn't help but notice.

Remember, confidence is the by-product of being unapologetically true to who you are.

> **Reflection:** Is there a part of you that you've been hiding to fit in or avoid judgement? What situations tend to bring out this sense of unease? How might it feel to start honouring that part of yourself a little more each day?

Living authentically doesn't require drastic changes overnight. It's about finding small ways to express yourself more fully each day. Perhaps it's sharing a passion with a friend, dressing in a way that feels true to you or speaking up for something you believe in. Each small action moves you closer to living in alignment with your true self, and each step builds a foundation for genuine confidence.

TRUE CONFIDENCE BEGINS THE MOMENT YOU STOP TRYING TO BE SOMEONE ELSE AND START EMBRACING WHO YOU REALLY ARE.

Make peace with your flaws

Celebrating yourself doesn't mean you emphasise all your strengths and completely ignore your flaws. It's about creating a realistic and compassionate self-image: understanding that your flaws are part of you, but they don't define your worth, and perfection isn't the goal either.

The key is to recognise your flaws without letting them consume you. **It's about striking a balance: accepting yourself as you are while striving for growth in the areas that matter to you.** You don't need to be perfect, but you also don't need to settle.

YOU CAN BE A MASTERPIECE AND A WORK IN PROGRESS AT THE SAME TIME.

All perceived flaws can be divided into two categories:

1. Those to work on and change.
2. Those to accept and love.

I invite you to use the table below to list what you perceive to be your flaws, and designate them into either 1 or 2.

If you're struggling to decide which category they fit into, consider these questions: 'Does this flaw negatively impact my relationships or my well-being?' 'Is this something that, if changed, would significantly improve my life or happiness?' If so, I'd put those into 'work on and change'. Any flaws that aren't hurting anyone, they don't really matter, and they make you who you are – put them into 'accept and love'.

For example:

- Not always listening to other people's perspectives = 1. work on and change.
- Not being very good at sport = 2. accept and love.
- Not feeling healthy in body and mind = 1. work on and change.

Flaw	Category

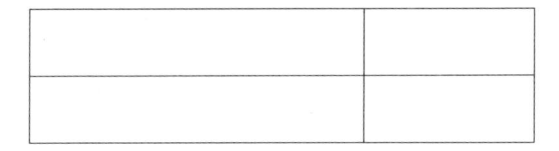

Remember that you're *not* allowed to accept *and* hate your flaws. This is a one-way ticket to low self-worth. Whether you work on and change your flaws, or you accept and love them, try to stop being so hard on yourself. We all have parts of ourselves that we struggle with, and it's important to recognise that imperfections are a universal part of being human.

Flaws are not just imperfections to be hidden or fixed; they often reveal deeper strengths. It's about changing how we see them. Instead of focusing only on the negative aspect of a flaw, try to see the positive side connected to it. For example, maybe you're not great at replying to messages promptly because you're someone who values being present when you're with others in person. Or perhaps you consider yourself overly cautious, but this means you're thoughtful and careful in your decisions, often preventing mistakes.

This isn't about denying your flaws or avoiding accountability – it's about shifting your perspective to find value in them. Reframing your flaws is important because it allows you to see the full picture of who you are: a person made up of both strengths and challenges, with each flaw contributing to your magnificent uniqueness.

✏️ EXERCISE: REFRAME YOUR PERSPECTIVE ON FLAWS

This exercise can transform the way you view yourself by helping you find the hidden strengths behind your flaws. Try it for yourself by filling out the table below. Start by identifying a disapproving thought you have about yourself, then reframe it by recognising the potential strength or positive quality that comes with it. I've included some examples to start you off.

Flaw	Strength
'I'm failing as a mum because I didn't pick up my son from school.'	'I'm succeeding as a mum because I'm providing for him and thinking about his future.'
'I'm always late, which means I'm unreliable.'	'I often take extra time to help others before I leave, which shows how much I care about people.'

HOW REFRAMING FLAWS HELPS US SEE OTHERS DIFFERENTLY

Reframing flaws in this way not only builds compassion for yourself but also strengthens your relationships. When you see the positive side of someone's 'flaw', you're more likely to appreciate them for who they truly are, flaws and all.

For example:

- Your partner might be indecisive at times, but that same quality could mean they're deeply considerate of others' feelings and want to make the best choice for everyone involved.
- A friend who seems overly talkative might have a gift for making others feel included.
- A family member who comes across as overly protective might simply love and care deeply.

The next time someone's quirks or imperfections bother you, pause and ask: what strength might this quality be connected to? This small shift can open up a whole new level of understanding, both in how you treat yourself and how you connect with others.

Embrace the 'slash'

How do you identify yourself? Are you a parent/caregiver, an athlete or a corporate employee? Identity is a fundamental part of the human experience – it allows us to nurture a sense of belonging and connection, helps us understand ourselves better and gives us a sense of purpose. But in life, we often feel pressured to define ourselves by a single role or title, and our need to identify with certain labels can end up restricting us.

What if we embraced the idea of being more than one thing? **What if we embraced the slash?**

If we only showed one side of who we are, we'd limit ourselves and prevent the world from seeing everything we have to offer. This tool is all about moving beyond the idea of identifying as just one thing and instead allowing yourself the freedom to be the multifaceted person you are. It's about proudly being this/that/and that too.

Imagine if Stanley Tucci had never embraced his passion for cocktails and cooking. He could have stayed 'just' an actor, but instead, he gave us his incredible TV shows and recipe books, opening a new dimension of his identity and creativity. Or take Dwayne 'The Rock' Johnson – what if he had stopped at wrestling? By leaning into his talents and curiosity, he became one of Hollywood's biggest stars and a global role model.

These examples remind us that embracing your 'slash' doesn't just add depth to your life – it can also unlock opportunities you never imagined. And while some slashes might bring new careers, that's not the goal for everyone. You don't have to make a major life change to embrace your 'slash': it's simply about living open-heartedly, indulging in your passions and throwing yourself into all the things that make you feel alive.

Every one of us is nuanced and multidimensional, and **there are countless versions of yourself waiting to be explored**. You can be a lawyer by day and a budding DJ by night. You can love boxing and still belt out Taylor Swift songs. You can be a mum who weight-lifts or a finance professional who writes poetry.

Your identity isn't defined by what pays the bills. Your value comes from who you are and what lights you up. You don't need permission or a pay cheque to call yourself a writer, an artist or a musician – if it brings you joy, it's part of who you are. So the next time someone asks, 'What do you do?', don't limit your answer to your day job. Tell them about your passions and interests too.

✏️ EXERCISE: WHAT'S YOUR SLASH?

Take a moment to reflect: what are the slashes that make up your identity? Write them down below. Celebrate them. And don't be afraid to keep adding more.

............../.............../.............../.............../...............

Embracing all of who you are is an ongoing journey. It's about acknowledging that you can be many things at once, and that each passion, hobby or quality adds depth to your identity. By embracing the 'slash', you give yourself the freedom to be the complex, interesting and wonderful person you were born to be.

FINAL WORDS

You. Are. Amazing.

The journey to building confidence and celebrating yourself is an ongoing one, but it's also incredibly rewarding. In this chapter, we've explored some of the biggest challenges that hold us back – whether it's our ingrained desire to be humble, the fear of coming across as arrogant or the lingering shame that stops us from embracing who we truly are.

But you are deserving of celebration. You are worthy of acknowledging your strengths, embracing your unique qualities and feeling proud of who you are, flaws and all. Self-celebration isn't about perfection; it's about recognising the value within you, seeing your progress and allowing yourself to take up space without fear.

Remember that confidence doesn't come from being the best or proving yourself to others – it comes from being true to who you are and accepting every part of your journey. It's about striking that balance between humility and pride, between striving for growth and accepting yourself as you are.

So, take the time to celebrate yourself. Reflect on how far you've come, nurture your passions, embrace your strengths and honour your unique journey. With every step you take towards self-acceptance and authenticity, you cultivate your confidence.

Don't wait for the big milestones. You are worth celebrating, today and every day.

STEP 6

DO HARD THINGS

Courage is not the absence of fear, but the willingness to act despite it.

ROXIE NAFOUSI — CONFIDENCE

As a parent, one of my greatest responsibilities – and privileges – is to nurture my son's confidence. Watching him grow into himself and seeing his self-belief blossom fills me with the most heart-warming sense of pride and joy.

I remember the first time he had to go on stage during an assembly at his new school. The class were singing 'Space Man' by Sam Ryder and, while many of the kids were animated, singing loudly and following along with the teacher's actions, Wolfe simply stood there, nervously scratching his head without singing a word. But when I returned to watch him in his end-of-year assembly several months later, it was a completely different experience. He hadn't suddenly become a star performer, but he was following along with some of the actions, smiling and singing at least half the words. I was so proud of how much his confidence had grown, especially doing something that clearly felt uncomfortable for him.

Kids naturally recognise the benefits of trying, even when they're not the best to begin with. They feel a sense of reward from learning and growing – it's instinctual because they're constantly starting from scratch with everything they do. As parents/caregivers, our role is to support and reinforce this willingness to try new things, helping young people build confidence by encouraging them to take on challenges, even when it feels daunting.

But as adults, we often forget the same lesson we teach our children. Instead, many of us hold ourselves back by shying away from things that seem scary, challenging or uncomfortable, and instead stick to what feels easy and comfortable.

Confidence isn't about avoiding discomfort – it's about trusting our ability to rise to the occasion, even when things get tough.

The avoidance of doing hard things can happen for several reasons:

1. **We accumulate negative and traumatic experiences:** We remember all the times we felt shame or embarrassment for doing something we weren't good at, reinforcing limiting beliefs.
2. **We have an increased awareness of risks:** As we get older, we think more rationally and logically, and we're more likely to avoid certain things because we understand the potential ramifications – whether they're financial, emotional, reputational or related to health and safety.
3. **We have more responsibility:** When we have families, careers and homes, the stakes feel higher if we're doing something that could lead to a negative outcome.
4. **Our stress response holds us back:** In a conversation on *RISE with Roxie*, neuroscientist and bestselling author Dr Tara Swart explained that elevated cortisol levels, the hormone associated with stress, make us less inclined to take risks. This response is an evolutionary mechanism intended to keep us safe from potential threats.
5. **Cognitive biases:** These tend to influence us more as we age. *Negativity bias*, in particular, becomes problematic, making negative experiences or

information weigh more heavily than positive ones. We may also fall into the cognitive distortion of *catastrophising*, which we met in Step 1: Master Your Thoughts (see page 31), where we focus excessively on potential threats and dangers instead of recognising possible rewards.

With that in mind, it makes sense that we have a tendency to avoid hard things. But, if we want to build true and lasting confidence, this is something we will have to overcome.

We've already discussed in Step 2: Act with Intention that confidence is something we build through action, and this includes when we take on challenges that push us beyond our comfort zones. When we face our fears, take on difficult tasks and do hard things, we prove to ourselves that we are capable, resilient and stronger than we might have believed.

The third step in my book, *MANIFEST*, is 'Align Your Behaviour' – here, I also speak about the importance of stepping outside your comfort zone to help you reach your goals. I included one of my favourite quotes: 'magic happens outside your comfort zone'. But, on reflection, the same applies for confidence: **confidence grows outside your comfort zone.**

TO STEP INTO YOUR FULL POTENTIAL,
YOU NEED TO SHOW YOURSELF THAT
YOU CAN DO HARD THINGS.

In this chapter, we'll explore how cultivating the right mindset can empower us to take on life's day-to-day challenges and we'll learn practical ways to embrace discomfort. But before we begin, I think it's worth reflecting on the fact that you've *already* faced and overcome many challenges in your life to get to where you are today, and those experiences are **proof of your resilience and strength.**

▶ EXERCISE: WHAT HAVE YOU ALREADY OVERCOME?

I encourage you to take some time to write down below all the times in your life when you tackled something stressful or difficult *and succeeded*. Think back to those moments that required strength, perseverance or courage. Here are a few examples to get you started:

- Starting a new job or career.
- Ending a toxic relationship or friendship.
- Standing up for yourself or others in a difficult situation.
- Learning a new skill or hobby that took time and patience.
- Healing from a breakup.
- Facing and overcoming a phobia such as public speaking.
- Managing a demanding work project or leading a team.
- Going through a challenging health journey, whether physical or emotional.

Things I've overcome:

....
....
....
....
....

Whenever you're confronted with a challenge, look back at your list to acknowledge everything you have already achieved and overcome. Remind yourself that you are more than capable of doing hard things.

THE GROWTH MINDSET

If we want to embrace challenges in order to strengthen our self-belief, we need to start by shifting our mindset. According to psychologist and professor Dr Carol Dweck, there are two types of mindset that determine how we approach challenges, motivate ourselves and strive towards success:[1]

1. **Fixed mindset:** We have this mindset when we believe that our intelligence and talents are defined and cannot be changed. We avoid challenges, give up easily and view effort as pointless because we believe we'll never be good enough anyway.
2. **Growth mindset:** When we have this mindset, we believe that our abilities and intelligence can be developed through hard work, learning and perseverance. We see challenges as opportunities to grow, we are more resilient in the face of setbacks and we view effort as more important than 'natural' ability. The more we believe in our ability to learn, the more willing we are to try hard things, which ultimately boosts our self-worth.

When we struggle with low self-esteem, we often find ourselves stuck in a fixed mindset. It can feel comfortable because it allows us to define our role in life and stick to it – we know our limitations, and we stay within them. But by creating such rigid boundaries, we restrict ourselves and limit our potential. Think of a fixed mindset like being stuck on a treadmill – you're moving, but you're not getting anywhere new. A growth mindset, on the other hand, is like exploring a new trail every day, with endless paths and opportunities to discover.

The way I see it, there are four key understandings that will help you develop a growth mindset:

1. We are all a work in progress.
2. Failure is our friend.
3. We can be comfortable in discomfort.
4. There is a domino effect of doing hard things.

Let's explore these in more detail now.

EMBRACE BEING A WORK IN PROGRESS

Somewhere along the way, many of us buy into this idea that, by a certain age, we're supposed to have everything figured out. We think we're supposed to be fully formed and that our skills, talents and potential are set in stone. But that's just not true. The reality is that we're never finished. We have the capacity to grow, learn and change at every stage of our lives.

Seeing ourselves as works in progress is the key to doing hard things. When we understand that we are constantly evolving, we realise that our current limitations are not permanent. **Instead of seeing challenges as reflections of our inadequacy, we start to see them as opportunities for growth.**

Think about how children approach learning new skills. Whether it's taking their first steps, learning to ride a bike or drawing a picture, they instinctively understand that they're works in progress. They don't expect to be perfect right away. They fall, they get up and they try again, fuelled by curiosity and persistence. Their innocent determination is something we can all learn from: it's not about being perfect; it's about showing up, trying and enjoying the process of getting better.

Starting my podcast, *RISE with Roxie*, was a perfect example of this. When Bauer Media first approached me with the idea, my immediate reaction was, 'Absolutely not.' Not because I didn't want to do it – deep down, I really did – but because I was terrified. I was afraid I wouldn't be a natural interviewer, that people would judge me and that I wouldn't measure up to the incredible podcasters already out there.

But then I paused and thought about what I'd tell any of you: if you're only saying no because you are afraid, it's all the more reason to do it. So, I took my own advice, stepped way outside of my comfort zone and said yes.

And you know what? The first three interviews were just as nerve-wracking as I'd feared. Watching the clips back, I cringe at my awkwardness and mistakes. But amid those moments, there were powerful ones, too. The guests shared wisdom and stories that I knew would resonate with listeners. By the fourth interview, I finally found a little bit of my rhythm and, with each interview that followed, I became more and more at ease.

Through this process, I learned two important lessons: firstly, that it was more than okay to be at the beginning of a journey and to be a work in progress, and secondly, that I didn't need to be perfect to be impactful. The most powerful moments in the podcast weren't the perfectly polished exchanges, but the raw, authentic ones. If I had let my fears keep me from taking that leap, *RISE with Roxie* wouldn't exist and I wouldn't have had the privilege of sitting down with incredible people, hearing their stories and sharing those conversations with the world. And beyond that, I wouldn't have experienced the profound growth that came from stepping into something that scared me.

Taking risks is not always easy, I know. It's uncomfortable, it's exposing and it can be unpredictable. But **each time we step into the unknown, we give ourselves the chance to discover something new about who we are and what we're capable of.**

TRUE CONFIDENCE IS NOT ABOUT NEVER FEELING AFRAID, IT'S ABOUT CHOOSING TO MOVE FORWARD IN SPITE OF IT.

When we see ourselves as works in progress, we give ourselves permission to be imperfect. This kind of self-acceptance doesn't just make it easier to face challenges, it also makes us more compassionate with ourselves. We stop worrying so much about not getting it right and we stop comparing ourselves to others, because we recognise that we are all on our own unique journeys, constantly evolving at our own pace.

SHIFT YOUR LANGUAGE

The way we talk to ourselves influences what we believe is possible. Using language that focuses on progress and possibility can change the way you see your challenges. It makes you more open to trying, learning and moving forward. So, **be mindful of your words**. They can be your biggest cheerleader or your biggest critic – choose the ones that help you move in the direction you want to go.

Instead of saying, 'I can't do it,' try adding a simple 'yet' at the end: 'I can't do it yet.' Or, even better, say, 'I'm working towards being able to do it.'

FAILURE IS YOUR FRIEND

I can't promise that you will succeed at everything you try. Sometimes, you will try and you *will* fail. But failure doesn't have to define you, crush your confidence or determine your worth. Instead, what if you changed your relationship with failure? What if you saw it not as a sign of defeat, but as an opportunity to grow, learn and redirect yourself to where you are supposed to be?

I recently watched a video of Roger Federer, one of the greatest tennis players of all time, giving a speech. He said:

> '... perfection is impossible. In the 1,526 singles matches I played in my career, I won almost 80 per cent of those matches ... what percentage of *points* do you think I won? Only 54 per cent. Even top-ranked tennis players win barely more than half of the points they play. When you lose every second point on average, you learn not to dwell on every shot. You teach yourself to think, "I double faulted, it's only a point." When you're playing a point, it has to be the most important thing in the world and it is, but when it's behind you, it's behind you. This mindset ... frees you to fully commit to the next point ... with intensity, clarity and focus.'[2]

Federer's words beautifully illustrate what it means to embrace failure as part of growth. Even at the peak of his career, he understood that success isn't about never losing; it's about learning to lose, let go and move forward.

Failure isn't the end of the story; it's simply a step along the way. It's normal to feel disappointed, but dwelling on failure only holds us back.

Take my client who opened an interiors store. She was passionate about design, but, eventually, the costs of running a physical store began draining her finances. She made the tough decision to close it and took her business online. Instead of letting this setback destroy her confidence, she adapted – learning to manage her resources better and reach a wider audience. It wasn't easy, but she found value in the experience and used those lessons to succeed in her next venture.

True growth happens when we stumble, learn and keep moving forward. This resilience is what ultimately allows us to build genuine, lasting confidence.

In my own career, I've experienced my fair share of failures. After the success of my first two books, I wrote something close to my heart – a manifestation book for kids aged seven to twelve. I felt sure it would resonate, but, in the end, it didn't sell nearly as well as my other books. A past version of myself would've called this a failure, but I refuse to see it that way. I'm proud of *MANIFEST for Kids*, and if it helps even one child, that is enough for me.

Failure doesn't mean you're not capable or not good enough. Success is never a straight path. It takes time, effort and learning to navigate setbacks, rejection and detours. In case you still need more proof of this, here are some of the most renowned success stories and some of the failures they faced along the way:

- Walt Disney was fired from a newspaper job because his editor thought he 'lacked imagination'. He went on to create one of the most successful entertainment companies in the world.
- Steven Spielberg was rejected twice by the University of Southern California School of Cinematic Arts. He became one of the most successful filmmakers in history.
- Lady Gaga was dropped by her first record label after only three months, but went on to become a multi-Grammy and Oscar-winning musician.
- Oprah Winfrey was fired from her first TV job as an anchor. She became one of the most influential talk-show hosts in history.
- Michael Jordan was cut from his high-school varsity basketball team and relegated to the junior team instead. He became one of the greatest players of all time.

HOW TO DEAL WITH FAILURE: A STEP-BY-STEP GUIDE

Here is my simple step-by-step guide to help you the next time you are faced with failure:

1. **Acknowledge the failure:** Accept it, without blaming yourself or others. Simply acknowledge that it happened.
2. **Give yourself permission to feel:** You're allowed to feel sad, frustrated or embarrassed. Write down your feelings or talk to someone you trust.
3. **Analyse what went wrong:** Reflect on why it happened. What factors contributed to the failure? What could you do differently next time?
4. **Reframe the failure as a lesson:** View it as a stepping stone towards growth. Ask yourself: what can I learn from this?
5. **Create a plan for development:** Will you try a new approach? How can you use what you've learned to grow?
6. **Be kind to yourself:** Don't let your inner critic take over. Instead, be your own cheerleader.
7. **Move on:** Let go of the failure and keep moving forward.

GET COMFORTABLE WITH DISCOMFORT

Most of life's greatest achievements come with some level of discomfort. Think about the moments you've felt most proud – passing an exam, stepping into a new role, giving birth, renovating a house or running a marathon. Those experiences required effort, uncertainty and, often, struggle. But that's what made the sense of achievement so rewarding.

Discomfort is a part of most new or challenging situations. It's that elevated heart rate before giving a presentation, the uncertainty before making a big decision or the vulnerability of trying something different. Instead of seeing discomfort as a threat, we need to recognise it as a sign of growth – a signal that we're stepping into something meaningful.

By allowing ourselves to sit with discomfort rather than avoid it, we create an opportunity for us to *level up and evolve*. Every time we do something uncomfortable and overcome the urge to quit or run away, we not only build our confidence, but we are rewarded – life will always bring us something great on the other side.

Stretch your comfort zone

In recent years, cold plunges have become a popular wellness trend, not just for their physical benefits, but for their ability to train our minds to stay calm under stress. When you step into freezing cold water, your instinct is to panic. However, with practice, you can learn to remain composed by focusing on slow, deep breaths, which helps calm your nervous system. This practice can have powerful effects beyond just that moment: when you learn to stay calm during extreme discomfort, you teach yourself how to handle stress better in everyday life.

Similarly, if we regularly challenge ourselves with small, uncomfortable tasks, we train our minds to stay calm during bigger challenges. This is about gradually expanding our comfort zones, or building our tolerance for discomfort, so that, when truly difficult moments arise, we are already equipped to face them with greater ease and composure.

I encourage you to come up with small, manageable challenges that help you lean into discomfort. Here are some ideas:

- **Cold showers:** Practise taking a cold shower for 30 seconds to a minute each day. It's an effective way to train your body and mind to remain calm in an uncomfortable situation.
- **Speak up:** If you usually stay quiet during meetings, try sharing your thoughts at least once. It might feel uncomfortable at first, but it's a powerful way to challenge yourself.
- **Try something new:** Join a class or start a hobby that you've always wanted to try but have avoided because it felt intimidating – like public speaking, dance or a new fitness activity.

The goal is not to overwhelm yourself, but to slowly stretch your comfort zone. **The more you learn to tolerate discomfort, the more confident you become – not because the discomfort disappears, but because you realise you can handle it.**

Reframe nerves as excitement

Another way to transform discomfort is to reframe it, especially when it shows up as nerves. I remember the first time I was invited to go on live TV in America. I was going on *The Today Show*, which was a huge opportunity for me and one that had been on my vision board. But I was *so* nervous. My stomach was in knots, my palms were sweaty and I kept thinking, 'What if I mess up? What if I forget what I want to say?'

Then, I reminded myself that nerves and excitement feel almost identical in the body. It's all about how we choose to interpret those sensations. So instead of saying, 'I'm so nervous,' I consciously told myself, 'I'm so excited to share my message with so many people.' Reframing those feelings made all the difference, and it worked!

The next time you feel nervous – whether it's about an important interview or going on a date – try reframing it as excitement. Say to yourself, 'I am excited for what's coming,' and imagine that your body is preparing you to step up and give your best. And remind yourself that even if things don't work out as planned, that's okay – it's all part of the journey. By channelling nervous energy into excitement and motivation, we can use it as fuel rather than letting it hold us back.

> DISCOMFORT, WHEN APPROACHED WITH THE RIGHT MINDSET, CAN BECOME ONE OF THE MOST POWERFUL FORCES FOR GROWTH IN OUR LIVES.

VISUALISATION AND MENTAL REHEARSAL

One powerful way to boost confidence before doing something challenging is to visualise yourself succeeding at it. Many world-renowned athletes and performers use visualisation techniques to mentally prepare and enhance their performance, and you can use the same approach in your own life.

Before you take on a difficult challenge, take a few minutes to close your eyes and imagine yourself successfully completing it. Picture yourself feeling calm, focused and capable. Visualise every detail: how your body feels, what the environment looks like, how you react to different situations and, most importantly, the sense of pride and accomplishment you'll feel once it's done. The more vividly you can imagine this, the more effective it will be.

> By mentally rehearsing success, you're training your brain to become familiar with the idea of succeeding, which helps reduce anxiety and boosts your confidence when you actually take on the challenge. This practice helps bridge the gap between where you are and where you want to be, setting you up to face hard things with a stronger sense of belief in yourself.

THE DOMINO EFFECT OF DOING HARD THINGS

There's something incredibly empowering about doing something we didn't think we could do. The sense of achievement that follows rewrites our internal narrative from 'I can't do this,' to 'I did this, and I can do even more.'

Psychologist Albert Bandura called these **mastery experiences** – moments that allow us to see our true strength.[3] These experiences provide tangible proof that we can handle whatever comes our way. They help build what Bandura termed **self-efficacy** – our belief in our ability to succeed in specific situations. Each mastery experience fuels this self-belief, creating a domino effect: as our self-efficacy grows, our confidence grows, making us more resilient and willing to take on future challenges.

Just as leaning into discomfort helps us grow more comfortable with it, taking on hard things expands our confidence. Each time we face a challenge, we strengthen our belief in our own capabilities, creating a foundation for tackling bigger challenges ahead.

The beauty of mastery experiences is that they are cumulative. It's not about needing to take on monumental tasks or changing our entire lives overnight, it's about starting with something small. Maybe that's committing to running a mile when you've never been a runner or attending a networking event alone when you usually take a friend for support. Each of these moments, no matter how seemingly small, is an opportunity to prove to yourself that you can grow, change and achieve.

The more you do hard things, the more you believe you can handle anything. **It's a cycle of growth – of testing your limits, learning from those experiences and expanding your belief in what you're capable of.** This is the domino effect of doing hard things: one success sets the foundation for the next.

✏️ EXERCISE: SET YOURSELF CHALLENGES

The key to triggering the domino effect lies in celebrating every step along the way. We often overlook our wins, especially the small ones we achieve every day. Yet these 'micro-challenges' have a cumulative effect that significantly impacts our self-worth and confidence.

Consider setting small daily goals that nudge you just outside your comfort zone – enough to challenge you, but not so much that they feel overwhelming. Each time you complete one of these challenges, you're proving to yourself that you can face discomfort and push through it.

Journal prompt: document your wins
Every time you take on a challenge, reflect on the experience with these prompts:

- How did I feel before I started?
- How did it feel while I was doing it?
- What did I learn?

- How did it feel once it was done?
- What does that feeling motivate me to want to do next?

When you look back at your entries, you'll see just how much you've accomplished. It's a tangible reminder that you can do hard things – and that you're always capable of more than you realise.

Confidence isn't always built in leaps and bounds; often, it's built in the quiet, everyday moments when you choose to take one small step forward. By tackling challenges, no matter how small, you create a domino effect of growth. Every step you take adds to your sense of self-belief, making you braver, stronger and more resilient with each passing day.

So, the next time you face something difficult, remind yourself: this is an opportunity to grow.

> ### EMBRACE THE NEW
>
> One powerful way to build confidence is to expose yourself to fresh and unfamiliar experiences.
>
> I recently spoke to Tali Sharot – a neuroscientist, professor and author – about why our brains tend to get bored easily and why novelty is so crucial for our wellbeing. New experiences not only stimulate our minds, but also boost our sense of competence.
>
> If you consider yourself a creature of habit, introduce novelty into your life in small, manageable ways. Start by trying something new every day, even if it's simple. Take a different route to work, try a cuisine you've never tasted before or watch a genre of movie you wouldn't usually pick. Each day, jot down what you tried and how it felt.

FINAL WORDS

OUR POWER LIES IN SEEING OUR POTENTIAL AS LIMITLESS.

I want to share a personal example of a time I had to push through something difficult and the profound effect it had on my confidence:

It was a Saturday, and I was at my sister's house sitting in the guest bedroom writing this very book, Step 5 to be exact. My sister was sitting next door with our kids, when suddenly I heard her panicked voice. I rushed in. She was on FaceTime to our housekeeper, Kiki, in Dubai. Kiki had been calling out to my dad to get him to wake up from his nap, but there was no response. We told her to go into the room, with us on FaceTime, and to try to wake him. I'll never forget her screams and hysteria, while my sister and I sobbed as we realised that our incredible and wonderful father had left this earth.

I was due to see him just two days later, as, on that Monday, I was flying to Dubai to do my MANIFEST: Live shows. I flew to Dubai, as intended, but, on Tuesday morning, instead of preparing for the show, I went with my mum and siblings to bury his body in an Islamic funeral. Hours later, I drove to the theatre and I went ahead with the show. It was, without doubt, the hardest show I've ever done. I was completely numb and I used every ounce of energy I had to deliver a performance that I hoped people would genuinely enjoy and benefit from.

When I got into the taxi afterwards, I felt drained and dejected. My inner critic grew loud, focusing on the moments when I messed up my lines and lost my flow. I felt angry with myself that I hadn't given my best performance, and I beat myself up over it.

The next morning, I had a word with myself. I realised that even though it hadn't been the best show I'd ever done, *I did do my best*. Despite what I'd been through that day, I still showed up, and I got through it. As I reframed my perspective, I immediately felt a wash of pride come over me. I felt proud of myself for doing something hard, and that feeling was so empowering and motivating. When I got back on stage that night for the second time, it felt incredible. I enjoyed every moment, with the added feeling that my dad was there beside me, cheering me on. That feeling of pride had given me a renewed sense of confidence that has stayed with me ever since.

Afterwards, I kept hearing friends and family saying, 'Gosh, I don't know how you did it.' But I know how: over the last few years, I have been constantly pushing myself out of my comfort zone. I've been doing things that scare me, make me feel vulnerable and push me to my limits. I've practised sitting through discomfort and facing challenges, and I've seen, first hand, how much growth I experience when I do that. I instilled a belief in myself that I could do hard things. So, when the time came, I trusted that I'd be able to handle it. And I did.

When we struggle with low self-esteem, it's easy to let fear and doubt rule our decisions. We question our abilities, tell ourselves we're not capable and stay within the safety of what's easy and familiar. But **when we stick to what's comfortable, we also miss out on the most exhilarating parts of life.** By avoiding hard things, we deny ourselves the huge sense of pride that comes from stepping into our potential. So, embrace challenges, whatever they may be.

Repeat after me, 'I can do hard things.'

STEP 7

BE OF SERVICE TO OTHERS

*When you pour into others,
you fill your soul with purpose.*

ROXIE NAFOUSI — CONFIDENCE

Low self-esteem can trap us in a relentless cycle of overthinking and self-criticism. We become hyper-focused on our perceived flaws, insecurities and how we appear to others, and overanalyse even the smallest things we've said or done. It's exhausting, and it keeps us locked inside our own heads, consumed by negativity.

I know this first hand because I've been there. At my lowest point, my life felt like it revolved around my problems, my fears and my inadequacies. I was stuck in an internal loop – a way of existing that felt small, isolating and dark. But through that experience, I discovered something that changed everything: **the best way to escape my own self-hatred was to channel my energy into helping others**.

Just before I became pregnant with Wolfe, I decided to start something I called 'Agony Aunt Sundays' on my Instagram. I put a question box in my stories, inviting my followers to share their dilemmas with me. I'd always been told I had a knack for giving advice, and I wanted to offer something meaningful – something that wasn't about highlight reels or the unrealistic perfection so often displayed on social media. At the time, my following was small, but I was beginning to build a community of people who cared about the same things I did.

Then, a week later, I found out I was pregnant, and I was plunged into the worst emotional low I had ever experienced. I hadn't even heard of prenatal depression before, but it hit me with an unrelenting force. Some people say that everyone goes through a 'dark night of the soul' at some point in their life, and this was definitely mine. I cried constantly, I lost my sense of self and what little self-esteem I had shattered entirely. It got to the point where I refused to leave the house for months, and getting through each day felt unexplainably overwhelming. And yet, every Sunday, I returned to Instagram to offer my advice to others. People wrote to me with questions about their relationships, their families and their careers. And by focusing on their problems, I was able to escape my own – if only for a little while.

This simple act of listening, and trying to help others, became my lifeline. When I couldn't look at myself in the mirror or bear to go outside, Agony Aunt Sundays gave me a reason to keep going. It was something beyond my own struggle – a small thread of purpose in a sea of despair. And, to my surprise, it started to grow. More people sent me their dilemmas each week, and I began receiving messages from those who had taken my advice and found it helpful. Slowly but surely, as Agony Aunt Sundays grew, so did my confidence.

I started to think: *maybe I'm not so useless. Maybe I do have something valuable to offer.* Helping others during my darkest days played a crucial role in guiding me to where I am today, to the work I do now and to the person I've become. It taught me that we can find meaning even in our hardest moments – especially when we use those moments to help lift someone else.

FEELING VALUED, NEEDED AND RESPECTED ARE CORNERSTONES OF CONFIDENCE.

When we believe that we have something to offer the world, it gives us a deep sense of purpose and belonging – both of which are essential to our well-being. When we can be of service to others, we counteract the limiting beliefs that tell us we're 'useless' or 'worthless'. Acts of kindness remind us that life is bigger than our insecurities, and they give us tangible proof of our value.

It might sound harsh, but one of the most liberating realisations is that **not everything is about us**. When we redirect our energy towards others – when we show up for our friends, our family or even complete strangers – we're freed from the suffocating grip of our own self-doubt. We remember that the world is vast, and that each of us has an important place within it. By stepping outside of ourselves, we regain perspective and, in doing so, we can find a renewed sense of gratitude.

WHY DOING GOOD BOOSTS OUR CONFIDENCE

I'm sure you'll already know, instinctively, that it feels good to do good. And this feeling is backed up by science. In psychology, acts of service are often described as **prosocial behaviours**.[1] These are behaviours that are intended to benefit others and the world around us. Prosocial behaviours include:

- Helping – for example, carrying a neighbour's heavy shopping.
- Sharing – for example, books or toys.
- Donating, whether money or things.
- Volunteering your time to help a cause or person.
- Cooperating with others in a task.
- Showing care for animals and the environment.
- Emotional support – for example, listening to someone, encouraging and reassuring them.

When we see how much these behaviours benefit others, *we benefit in return*. Neuroscience has shown that when we engage in prosocial behaviours, the brain releases chemicals like endorphins, oxytocin, dopamine and serotonin, which are associated with happiness, stress relief and improved mood. This feeling is known as the 'helper's high', because it elevates happiness and combats depression.[2]

But even more than simply providing a quick hit of happiness, prosocial behaviour can help us to build our self-esteem. This happens for several different reasons:

It shifts our focus away from ourselves

You've probably noticed that when you help someone else with a problem they're having, it can be a welcome distraction from anything that you might be going through at the time. Research on empathy supports this: one study from 2006 explored how empathy improves emotional regulation by redirecting cognitive resources away from personal stressors.[3]

I have a friend who often calls me for advice and, when she does, she can easily speak non-stop for an hour, giving me every detail of her latest dilemma without asking a single question about my life. And honestly? I love it. I genuinely enjoy listening to and helping her, and it always provides a much-needed break from my own stress and responsibilities.

We improve our self-perception

When we perceive ourselves as good people, we feel better about who we are. Recent research discovered that altruistic behaviour (a type of prosocial behaviour that we do without expecting anything in return) can enhance positive self-perception.[4] When individuals perceive themselves as helpful and compassionate, it boosts their self-image and confidence. This positive reinforcement creates a cycle where feeling good about oneself leads to more prosocial behaviour, therefore enhancing self-esteem even further.

We feel a sense of accomplishment

In Step 6: Do Hard Things, we learned that succeeding in challenges boosts our self-esteem by improving our 'self-efficacy' (our belief in our abilities – see page 175). Research shows that engaging in prosocial behaviour has a similar impact, leading to increased feelings of competence. In a recent study, participants reported higher levels of self-efficacy after engaging in altruistic activities, which reinforced their sense of personal achievement and capability.[5]

We gain a sense of purpose and meaning

Purpose can mean different things to different people, but, to me, it's about having a mission greater than yourself – something that fuels your drive and motivates you to persevere through challenges. For me, purpose is what gives meaning to my actions, providing a sense of clarity and direction.

A 2015 study found a clear link between altruistic behaviour and a greater sense of purpose. Researchers asked 400 participants how often they engaged in acts of kindness, including volunteering. They discovered that those who were more altruistic reported a stronger sense of purpose and meaning in their lives.[6]

It makes us feel connected to others

Acts of kindness, whether it's smiling at a stranger, holding a door open or helping a friend, create small but meaningful moments of connection. Research shows that prosocial behaviour provides opportunities for positive social interactions, boosting our mood and overall well-being.[7] When we feel connected to others, we increase our sense of belonging, which ultimately enhances how we see ourselves.

Moments of connection – whether with friends or strangers – are crucial, especially because we live in an increasingly lonely world. Although it might seem like we're constantly connecting with others online, these interactions often lack the depth of real-life connections and can leave us feeling even more isolated. In a UK survey from June 2023, 26 per cent of adults reported feeling lonely often, always or sometimes.[8] This matters because research has shown a correlation between loneliness and low self-esteem.[9] On the other hand, when we feel socially connected, our self-esteem naturally flourishes.

It reduces social anxiety

Doing kind things can significantly reduce social anxiety. In a 2013 study, participants who performed kind acts reported lower levels of social anxiety and higher levels of happiness and self-esteem.[10] Kind acts help counteract the negative assumptions that often fuel social anxiety, such as 'people are judging me' or 'people don't like me'. When we do something kind for others and receive a positive response, it challenges those distorted thoughts and replaces them with more positive, evidence-based beliefs.

Moreover, focusing on what we can do for others shifts our attention from worrying about how we're perceived to something we have control over – our actions. This not only helps us feel more comfortable in social situations, but also empowers us with a greater sense of agency.

It encourages gratitude

Helping others gives us a broader perspective on our own problems and challenges. When we recognise that we're in a position to help someone else, it also makes us aware that we are in a place of privilege, even if we don't always see it that way. This realisation shifts how we see ourselves and what we have, helping us move away from focusing on what we lack.

During the Q&A sessions in my events and workshops people often share their struggles with the room. Sometimes they're dealing with profound loss, a breakup, illness or other hardship.

In these moments of vulnerability, something beautiful happens. There's a palpable feeling in the room – an energy that comes from the empathy and compassion everyone feels. People listen intently, nod in understanding, and often shed tears together. It's a reminder of our shared humanity, and it creates this incredible sense of connection among everyone in the room. In those moments, I know that everyone listening is also taking a moment to appreciate their own lives more deeply and feel grateful for what they have.

It's important to note that just because others are facing hardships, it doesn't mean our own struggles aren't valid. However, helping others can be a powerful way to shift our perspective. It helps us focus on the good that's present in our lives, even when things aren't perfect. By tapping into our compassion and empathy, we remember what truly matters.

In helping others, we're not just giving to them – we're reminding ourselves of our own capacity for kindness, resilience and the importance of gratitude. And ultimately, this helps us see ourselves in a more positive light.

FIND THE RIGHT BALANCE

Before we go any further, I want to make one point clear: **being of service to other people should never mean sacrificing yourself.**

In the same way that being of service to other people helps us in return, it's also true that when we help ourselves, we're better equipped to be of service to others. I know that I am a better mum, partner, boss and friend when I also make time for myself. When we fill our own cups, we gain more energy and resources to fill other people's cups too.

> It's all about finding the right balance between being of service to others and being of service to ourselves. Both can, *and should,* work together. It is not either/or.
>
> When you are being of service to others, make sure to ask yourself these key questions:
>
> - Have I also looked after myself today?
> - Am I giving myself the same support and care I give to other people?
> - Will this put my own well-being at risk? Or will it boost it?
>
> By being mindful of these questions, we can ensure that our efforts to help others don't come at the expense of our own health and happiness. Serving others is most meaningful when it comes from a place of abundance, not emptiness.

HOW TO BE OF SERVICE

When we think about being of service, we often picture charity work or giving up a huge amount of our time and resources for a cause. While those forms of giving are impactful, being of service can take many forms – let's explore some of these now.

Do what you can

The chances are, you're already being of service without realising just how much value you're providing. Take, for example, your day job. Let's say you're a salesperson. You might think, 'I'm just selling products to make a profit.' But think about what you're actually doing for your customers. You're helping someone find the right solution to a problem they have – whether that's helping them choose a product that fits their needs or making sure they understand all of their options. You're making their life easier and adding value by guiding them through a decision they may have found difficult on their own. That's being of service.

In my career, I have a very clear mission in mind: I want to help people live their best, most fulfilled lives and feel the most empowered they can be. This is the sense of purpose that drives me forward.

I'm lucky that I work in an industry where I can see the impact I'm having because people will so often tell me directly by messaging me on social media or when I meet them in person. I know how privileged and honoured I am to experience this. However, in many careers, you might struggle to see how and why you're making a difference. But I want you to know that, **in whatever you spend your days doing, you are making a difference**.

Every job has elements of service, even if it's not so obvious and direct. If you're a barista, you're giving people their morning caffeine fix (and if you greet them with a smile, you might just make their morning). If you work as a financial adviser, you're helping people protect their finances to give them more freedom in the future. And whether you're a cashier who makes someone's day with a smile, a customer service representative solving issues or a team leader who motivates and supports your colleagues, you're positively impacting others.

Being of service also includes:

- Giving advice to friends.
- Picking up your kids from school every day.
- Visiting your elderly parents and helping them around the house.

- Mentoring junior colleagues at work.
- Cooking dinner or doing the washing up.
- Helping a customer navigate a tough decision.
- Checking in on your neighbours.
- Feeding and caring for local wildlife.

Remember, purpose doesn't have to exist solely in a work setting. It can also mean:

- Raising confident and happy kids.
- Caring for the environment.
- Contributing to your community.
- Being a reliable friend or family member.
- Pursuing you passions.

When we start to see the service in our everyday actions, we begin to appreciate ourselves more. Acknowledging the good you're already doing helps you recognise the impact you have on others.

➤ EXERCISE: REFLECT ON YOUR VALUE

1. **List your acts of service:** In the space below, write down all the ways you're already of service in your life. Consider how you support your family and friends, acquaintances, neighbours, colleagues and even strangers.

   ....
   ....
   ....

2. **Consider how you feel:** Now, reflect on how these actions also make you feel. Do you feel proud when a friend values and takes your advice? Do

you feel a sense of connection when you help your neighbour?

....
....
....

3. **Enhance the benefits:** Is there a way to enhance these confidence-boosting benefits? Where and how could you expand these opportunities to feel even more fulfilled?

But always remember . . . you can't do everything.

In our hyperconnected world, we're bombarded with information about all the struggles happening globally. It can make us feel overwhelmed and helpless, as if we're never doing enough. But I want you to consider that you are only one person. You can't solve every problem, and carrying the weight of the world on your shoulders will only leave you exhausted, *which helps no one.*

There's also a lot of pressure on social media to be vocal about every issue, to support every cause publicly. I have a friend who is a passionate animal rights activist. He works tirelessly with dog rescues and animal charities, yet sometimes he feels guilty for not being more vocal about other causes. I always remind him: 'You're making a real difference where you focus your energy, and that matters.' Dedicating yourself fully to one cause often creates a much greater impact than spreading yourself too thin.

There are endless ways to make a positive impact – big or small. Don't let anyone make you feel guilty for what you're not doing. Focus on the good that you *are* doing, and remember that even small acts of service can have a powerful ripple effect.

Give praise freely

Even if you find it challenging to accept compliments yourself, you know how good it feels when someone notices your efforts, admires the outfit you carefully chose or appreciates your hard work. Compliments, praise and positive feedback are small but powerful acts of kindness – yet many of us hesitate to offer them. We might feel embarrassed, worry about seeming 'too keen' or assume people already know what they're doing well. But by uplifting others, we send positive energy into the world – energy that often finds its way back to us.

The people who compliment others freely tend to be some of the warmest, most magnetic individuals. When we make it a habit to see the best in others, we not only brighten their day but also shift our own perspective to focus on positivity.

> A KIND WORD HAS THE POWER TO TRANSFORM SOMEONE'S DAY, GIVE THEM HOPE AND OFFER THE ENCOURAGEMENT THEY MIGHT NOT EVEN KNOW THEY NEED.

When you offer a compliment, make it thoughtful and genuine. Go beyond surface-level observations. What do you truly admire about that person? Is it their enthusiasm, their resilience in tough times or their sharp sense of humour? Maybe it's their creativity, their way of making others feel included or their ability to handle challenges with grace. These deeper acknowledgements don't just make compliments more meaningful, they also strengthen connections and cultivate a sense of mutual appreciation.

So, don't hold back. **The next time you notice something admirable about someone, say it. You never know the impact your kind words might have – and the ripple effect they might create.**

Perform a random act of kindness

I was at my local supermarket recently and at the front of the queue was a young boy who had realised he'd forgotten his wallet just as he was about to pay. Without hesitation, the person behind him stepped forward and offered to cover the bill. It wasn't a huge amount, but it was such a generous and heart-warming act, and I could see how relieved and grateful the boy was.

We all know how special it feels to be on the receiving end of an act of kindness – whether it's from someone you love or a complete stranger – but what we often underestimate is just how powerful it is to be the one giving.

In a study from 2005, participants were asked to perform five random acts of kindness each week for six weeks.[11] The study found that individuals who performed these acts reported higher levels of happiness and well-being compared to a control group. Although the study focused on well-being, the boost in happiness often correlates with improved self-esteem and confidence. By shifting our focus away from our own concerns and offering something meaningful to others, we are reminded of our ability to create positive change in someone else's life – and that is an empowering feeling.

These small gestures require very little effort, but the rewards are incredible. Remember that when we engage in acts of kindness, our brains release feel-good chemicals. This natural boost in mood doesn't just help us feel happier in the moment, it also helps to reduce stress, alleviate anxiety and improve our overall sense of self-worth. This is why a simple act of kindness can act as a quick fix to feel like we're adding value to the world and reinforcing our belief that we matter.

The ripple effect of kindness is also something worth noting. When you perform an act of kindness, you're not just impacting the person receiving it – you're also inspiring others who witness it. In fact, research found that witnessing acts of kindness creates a 'moral elevation' that makes people more likely to engage in altruistic behaviour themselves.[12] This means that **kindness is contagious**, and it encourages others to pay it forward, creating a positive chain reaction that spreads far beyond that initial moment.

> THE MORE WE ENGAGE IN KINDNESS, THE MORE WE INSPIRE OTHERS TO DO THE SAME, ULTIMATELY UPLIFTING EVERYONE'S SENSE OF SELF-WORTH.

EXERCISE: PERFORM A RANDOM ACT OF KINDNESS EVERY DAY

I challenge you to perform at least one act of kindness every day. If you're not sure where to start, here are some suggestions:

- **Give a genuine compliment** to someone who looks like they need a confidence boost.
- **Hold the door open** for someone juggling bags, kids or coffee cups.
- **Buy a coffee for the person in the queue behind you** at your favourite café.
- **Leave a sticky note with an uplifting message** in a public place, like in a library book or on the mirror of a public toilet.
- **Offer to babysit or pet-sit** for a friend who could use a break.
- **Donate warm clothing or supplies** to a local shelter, especially during colder months.

- **Reach out to an old friend** you haven't spoken to in a while and ask how they're doing.
- **Write a thank you note** to someone who has positively impacted your life, like a teacher, colleague or mentor.
- **Bring in treats or snacks** to share with your co-workers.
- **Compliment a stranger's efforts**, like the shop assistant who went above and beyond.

Every small act of kindness you perform is a powerful reminder that you can make a difference and that your presence matters. Start small, but stay consistent, and watch how these acts of kindness ripple through your own life and the lives of those around you.

A NOTE ON RECIPROCITY

It can be disheartening when we help others and feel we get nothing in return – sometimes not even a simple 'thank you'. Feeling unappreciated can be tough, especially when we're putting effort into spreading kindness.

I know it's not easy, but I encourage you to take pride in doing good deeds without expecting anything in return. When we focus on what we can control – our actions – rather than what we can't – others' responses – we can find more peace. Remember, everyone is different; we all have our own priorities, values and experiences that shape how we behave. Lowering expectations for how others should respond can help protect us from disappointment.

That said, healthy relationships do require reciprocity. There will be times when one person needs more support, but, overall, there should be a balance. When we give too much without receiving, it can hurt our confidence and leave us feeling unworthy of the love and respect we give so freely.

If you find yourself in a partnership or friendship that feels one-sided – where you're always giving and rarely receiving – it might be time to re-evaluate the role that relationship plays in your life. You deserve the same love, respect and energy you give to others. Remember, just because someone isn't giving that to you, it doesn't mean you aren't worthy of it.

FINAL WORDS

Being of service to others is more than just a kind gesture; it's a profound way to remind ourselves of our value, our capacity to make a difference and the fact that life is far bigger than our insecurities.

When I began Agony Aunt Sundays, I never imagined it would change my life. It was a small gesture, something I could do during a time when I felt lost and defeated. Yet, as I showed up week after week, offering advice and helping others, I discovered a spark of purpose. Gradually, I began to see myself in a new light. My confidence grew, and so did my belief that I had something meaningful to contribute.

You have something to offer too. No matter what challenges you face, there is always a way to make an impact – big or small. Helping others gives us perspective. It reminds us that we matter, cultivates connection, purpose and gratitude, and shows us how valuable we truly are.

This isn't about grand gestures or sacrificing your own needs; it's about creating genuine moments of connection – with friends, family, strangers or even yourself. It's about showing up, doing what you can and recognising that every kind word, every thoughtful action, counts. It's also about finding balance and nurturing yourself, so you can continue to uplift others without losing your own sense of well-being.

When you step into the space of giving, you discover a beautiful truth: **the more we lift others, the more we rise ourselves**. It's in those moments of service that we truly understand our worth. So, go out there. Do good. Be kind. And remember, you're already making a difference – in ways you might not even realise yet.

STEP 8

SHOW UP AS YOUR BEST SELF

You owe it to yourself to become everything you've ever dreamed of being.

ROXIE NAFOUSI — CONFIDENCE

We have reached the final step of my eight-step guide to confidence. This step is all about stepping into the character of your most confident self. It's about walking the walk and showing up as the person you want to become.

In my *MANIFEST* books, I emphasise the importance of stepping into the character of your future self. I use the phrase 'fake it till you become it' – the idea is to embody the identity of the person you aspire to be, starting today. By acting like your best self, you start to embody those qualities until they become second nature. It's not about pretending to be someone you're not; **it's about aligning your actions with the most empowered version of yourself and bringing that version of you to life.**

This concept is backed by psychological research. In the 1970s, social psychologist Daryl Bem introduced 'Self-Perception Theory', which suggests that we shape our beliefs about ourselves by observing our own actions.[1] For example, if you consistently step up to help others in challenging situations, you begin to see yourself as reliable and capable. Similarly, when you act with confidence, over time, you'll start to genuinely believe you are confident.

We can use this principle to our advantage. Imagine you're given the opportunity to lead a team at a work conference, and your first instinct is to panic. Perhaps you think you're not a natural leader or maybe you've had uncomfortable experiences in the past. Instead of giving in to that panic, choose to step into the character of your future self. **Ask yourself, 'What would my most confident self do?'** Then, **embody** that confidence – push through the nerves, introduce yourself, ask questions and engage with others.

As you do this, you'll often find the experience becomes more enjoyable and you start to genuinely feel comfortable. Over time, these small actions add up, and suddenly you realise you're no longer pretending – you've actually become the confident person you wanted to be.

Acting the part is one of my favourite ways to overcome self-doubt. When you decide to show up confidently, you begin to feel it *and others* begin to see it in you, too.

With this in mind, let's explore some practical strategies to help you show up as your most confident self, no matter the situation:

1. Master your body language.
2. Communicate effectively and assertively.
3. Trust in your own decisions.
4. Do it yourself.
5. Use visualisation.
6. Dress the part.
7. Get comfortable setting boundaries.

MASTER YOUR BODY LANGUAGE

It's incredible just how much we communicate without actually saying anything. The psychologist Albert Mehrabian developed a model in the 1960s that suggested that non-verbal communication accounts for the majority of how we interpret messages in face-to-face communication.[2] According to his model,

55 per cent of communication is conveyed through body language, 38 per cent through tone of voice and *only 7 per cent through the actual words spoken.*

Today, researchers have continued to explore the significant role of non-verbal cues in how we communicate. Behavioural investigator Vanessa Van Edwards, bestselling author of *Cues* and *Captivate*, has shown that positive body language – such as eye contact, open gestures and an upright posture – helps people to not only make good first impressions, but also *feel more confident themselves*.[3] Her findings demonstrate that the way we move and hold ourselves not only shapes how others perceive us, but also sends powerful signals to our own minds, directly influencing our internal sense of confidence.

EMBODIED COGNITION EFFECT

The 'embodied cognition effect' is the idea that our bodies and our emotions are closely linked. It suggests that our body language doesn't just reflect our emotions – it can actively shape them. For example, standing in a confident posture (often called a 'power pose') can help you *feel* more confident, even if you weren't feeling that way initially.

This concept highlights how closely linked our minds and bodies are, and how **consciously changing our physical state can have a positive impact on our mental state.**

Amy Cuddy, social psychologist and author of *Presence*, suggests that adopting a 'power pose' for just two minutes each day can increase feelings of confidence and reduce stress.[4]

Before heading into a situation where you feel in need of a confidence boost, try one of her power poses, as outlined in her viral 2015 Ted Talk:

1. **The Wonder Woman (or Superman) pose:** Stand with your feet shoulder-width apart and place your hands on your hips. Your chest is open, with your chin slightly raised, creating an assertive and powerful stance.
2. **The victory pose:** Stand with your arms raised above your head in a wide V-shape. This pose is similar to athletes who celebrate victory or triumph.

I know, first hand, how much body language can impact not just how we are perceived, but how we feel. Not too long ago, I gave a keynote talk on my '7-Step Guide to Manifesting' – a workshop I've done countless times and feel incredibly confident delivering. But, on this occasion, I was wearing an outfit that was extremely restrictive: I couldn't raise my arms above chest height because, if I did, the top would lift up in the wrong place and reveal a little too much skin. As a result, I was unable to express myself the way I typically do – no open arm movements, no enthusiastic gestures and no big welcoming wave as I stepped on stage. Throughout the talk, I felt a difference in my energy and, afterwards, I felt dejected, wondering what had gone wrong. Then I realised, *it was my body language*, restricted and subdued, that must have sent signals to my mind, suggesting that I wasn't fully open or confident, and ultimately affecting how I felt throughout the talk.

To help you physically step into the character of your most confident self, on the next page are some simple yet impactful ways to adapt your body language.

Stand tall
When you're standing up, keep your back straight, with your shoulders relaxed but rolled back, and your chest slightly out. Imagine a string pulling you gently upwards from the top of your head.

While sitting, avoid slouching forward or leaning back. Plant both feet on the floor so that you feel grounded. Good posture not only looks confident, but also helps you feel balanced and strong.

Stay open
Keeping your arms uncrossed and your hands visible can help you feel more open and comfortable. In an episode of *RISE with Roxie*, body language expert Adrienne Carter (also known as 'The Face Whisperer') explained that having your hands visible during conversations also helps others to trust you more.

Avoid fidgeting
Nervous habits like tapping your feet or playing with your hair can increase feelings of anxiety. Reducing these habits helps you feel more in control and calm.

If you notice yourself fidgeting, consciously make an effort to pull your hands away. Instead, use your hands for purposeful gestures that can enhance the message of whatever you're saying. This will help you feel more in control of your movements.

Smile!
Smiling is an effective way to help you feel more relaxed and positive thanks to the endorphins it releases. It will also make those around you feel more comfortable, creating a positive feedback loop that boosts your own sense of ease. My dad always used to tell me to fake a smile or laugh when I was feeling down, and, as much as I resisted it at the time, he was right.

Adjust your vocal tone and pace
Speaking at a steady pace – taking pauses and breaths when you need to – helps you feel more grounded and in control. This, in turn, makes others more likely to listen and engage with what you're saying.

Keep a level head
I mean this literally. Keeping your chin slightly raised can help you feel more attentive and assertive. Tilting your head down too much can make you feel unsure, so keeping your head level supports a sense of confidence.

Take up space
I also mean this literally. When we feel insecure, we tend to shrink ourselves – both mentally and physically. Taking up more space can help you feel more assertive and powerful. Stand with your feet shoulder-width apart, avoid crossing your arms or legs tightly, and allow your body to occupy the space it needs. This stance helps you feel more grounded and confident.

Walk with intention
The way you move also plays a significant role in how confident you feel. Whether you're giving a presentation, walking into a meeting or entering a new environment, take purposeful strides and *walk with intention*. Avoid shuffling or moving too quickly, as this can make you feel nervous or on edge. Walking purposefully helps you feel more steady, self-assured and ready to take on anything.

Mastering your body language is the foundation of showing up as your best self – it signals confidence, not only to others, but to yourself. But body language alone isn't enough: to truly embody your confident self, you also need to communicate effectively.

COMMUNICATE EFFECTIVELY AND ASSERTIVELY

Effective communication allows us to express our thoughts, needs and feelings clearly, creating more positive connections with other people and making us feel more in control in both our personal and professional lives.

Research supports the impact of good communication skills on confidence. One study on communication apprehension found that people who can articulate their thoughts effectively are less likely to experience anxiety in social settings.[5] It also showed that expressing yourself clearly helps you engage more comfortably in conversations, which, over time, can boost your self-esteem and confidence.

In the 1990s, researchers studied the benefits of assertive communication training, and found that participants who took part in this training reported reduced stress levels *and increased confidence* in social interactions.[6]

Some of the skills for effective communication can be used across the board, but I'm going to divide them into two categories: **confident communication for everyday use** and **confident communication in difficult situations**.

Confident communication for every day

These tips will help you in all sorts of social scenarios – whether you're meeting new parents at the school gate, attending a work event or catching up with friends. Mastering these skills will not only help you make a positive impression, but also build your confidence in navigating social interactions.

Listen actively

When you focus on truly listening to what the other person is saying, you naturally shift your attention away from how you're coming across. My friend Josh Smith – a podcaster, journalist and author of *Great Chat: Seven lessons for better conversations, deeper connections and improved wellbeing* – always emphasises the importance of listening over talking. As he says, 'We have two ears and one mouth. Let that be your reminder to listen twice as hard.'

Josh often talks about the power of **active listening**, which involves making a conscious effort to fully understand someone and what they're saying. This means paying attention not only to their words, but also to their tone, body language and other non-verbal cues.

Active listening isn't just about staying silent; it's about engaging meaningfully. Avoid interrupting or trying to formulate a response while the other person is speaking. Instead, respond in a way that shows you were truly listening. For example, you could paraphrase what they said: 'So, what you're saying is . . .' or validate their experience with phrases like: 'That sounds amazing,' or 'That must have been really hard.' These responses make the other person feel valued and understood, while also helping you feel more in control of the conversation – a subtle but powerful confidence booster.

> ## AVOID 'ME, ME, ME LISTENING'
>
> Often, we instinctively share our own stories or examples while someone else is speaking. When done sparingly and empathetically, this can deepen connection. But be careful not to make the conversation about yourself. Josh calls this 'Me, me, me listening' – when you listen just to relate it back to your own experiences.

> Before sharing your story, ask yourself:
>
> - Will this make the other person feel reassured and seen?
> - Or will it take away from what they've just shared?

Don't be afraid to pause

Filling every gap in a conversation can sometimes signal nervousness. But natural pauses are, well, *natural* – and they can actually enhance the flow of a conversation. Getting comfortable with brief moments of silence is a subtle but powerful skill. I'm not talking about long, awkward silences, but just a couple of seconds. When someone finishes speaking, pause for two seconds before replying. This small gap gives you a moment to process their words and formulate a thoughtful response, which can make your interactions feel more intentional and composed.

Ask engaging questions

One of the best ways to keep a conversation flowing is to ask open-ended questions – those that invite more than a simple 'yes' or 'no' answer. Focus on 'how' and 'why' questions, which encourage the other person to elaborate and share more about themselves. For example, instead of asking, 'Do you like working in finance?' you could ask, 'How did you get started in your career?'

As Josh Smith explains in *Great Chat*, asking questions also enhances our emotional intelligence:

> 'It increases our understanding of others and makes us like ourselves more too, as we feel we are more engaged in our relationships and more interested in others – and that is good for the soul. As we increase our emotional

intelligence, we are more aware of the right questions to ask and when to ask them: [a] win–win.'

I love this insight because it ties back to what we explored in Step 7: when we act in service to others, we also act in service to ourselves.

If you're looking for more tips on how to feel confident in social situations, I highly recommend reading *Great Chat*. Josh's book has taught me so much about the art of conversation – from navigating small talk to building deeper, more meaningful connections.

Confident communication in difficult situations

In the last few years, some of the times I have felt most proud of myself are the times when I've been able to have difficult conversations, and managed to stay calm yet empowered when doing so. In the past, it definitely wasn't something I'd been good at; instead, I would either find myself becoming extremely defensive, reactive and emotional, or I would crumble and pander to the needs of others immediately. Both responses came from a place of insecurity, and both only reinforced those feelings further.

The tips below will help you feel a sense of authority when you're expressing your wants and needs in a difficult situation – for example, if you want to set a boundary with a friend or partner, or you have an important meeting with your boss to discuss your pay and development. Being assertive in these situations helps strengthen your confidence, ensuring that you feel in control and capable even during challenging interactions.

Take a breath and pause

Before responding, especially in a high-pressure or emotional situation, take a moment to pause and breathe. This simple step can prevent you from reacting impulsively and saying something you may later regret. When emotions run high, it's easy to let anger or fear take over, but taking a breath gives you a moment to regain composure and respond thoughtfully rather than reactively.

DON'T REACT, RESPOND.

Use 'I' statements

This helps you communicate how you feel by taking ownership of your own perspective. Instead of saying, 'You never listen to me,' you can say, 'I feel unheard when I'm interrupted.' By using 'I' statements, you're able to clearly express yourself while reducing the likelihood of that other person becoming defensive.

Avoid filler words

When we feel unconfident, we tend to fill sentences with things like, 'maybe', 'just' and 'sort of'. When you're writing texts or emails, can you look over your messages and remove these types of words and phrases? Can you practise removing these words from your vocabulary in real-life settings too? Eliminating filler words can make you sound and feel more self-assured.

Clarify what you do want or need

Instead of saying 'I don't like' or 'I don't need', try using phrases like 'I prefer', 'I need', 'I expect' or 'I would like'. This shifts the conversation from complaints to solutions, making it more positive and productive. Clear communication helps others understand your needs better, reducing misunderstandings and fostering cooperation.

For example, instead of saying, 'I don't like it when meetings run late,' you could say, 'I prefer meetings that stay on schedule so I can manage my other responsibilities effectively.' This phrasing not only sets a clear boundary, but also communicates your desired outcome in a constructive way.

By focusing on what you *do* want rather than what you don't, you feel more empowered and direct the conversation towards actionable solutions. This approach reinforces your sense of agency and encourages more favourable outcomes for everyone involved.

Try the 'broken record' technique

This is an assertiveness technique that involves staying firm in your point without becoming aggressive. If someone pushes back on some kind of boundary you have, it can be easy to back down in order to avoid conflict. But instead, you can calmly repeat your point until it gets through. Maintain your stance with composure and respect.

Delay your response

When you're put on the spot, it can be easy to feel pressured into agreeing or making commitments that you may later regret. This often happens when we feel backed into a corner and want to avoid conflict. To prevent this, practise delaying your response. Instead of immediately agreeing, try phrases like, 'I need some time to think about it,' or 'I'll get back to you on that.'

By giving yourself this space, you allow yourself time to evaluate the request, consider your own needs and make a thoughtful decision that aligns with your priorities. It also communicates that you value your time and boundaries, which can lead to others respecting them as well.

DON'T BE AFRAID TO ROLE PLAY

When I anticipate an important meeting or conversation, I tend to practise what I want to say before I go in. Sometimes I do it in my head, sometimes aloud to

> myself and sometimes with another person I love and trust. While it might feel a little awkward at first, the more you can practise saying what you need to say assertively, the more confident you will feel when the moment arrives.

TRUST IN YOUR OWN DECISIONS

Decision-making is an essential aspect of confidence because it reinforces self-reliance and self-trust. When we struggle with low confidence, making decisions can be extremely hard: we lean heavily on others' opinions, we don't trust our own thought processes and we can end up doubting the decisions we've made and look back with regret.

To show up as the confident, capable version of you that you aspire to become, you must be able to trust yourself, the way you would trust someone you look up to.

I remember how, for the longest time, I would turn to my friends and family for help with every decision – whether it was something as small as what I should have for lunch or as big as whether or not I should break up with my boyfriend. I didn't trust my own judgement and I felt anxious about making the 'wrong' choice. It wasn't until I had a conversation with my mum about confidence that I began to understand the real impact of this.

My mum told me that growing up she was never allowed to make any decisions. Her parents were incredibly strict and she had no say in her life. She was told what to eat, how to dress, how to spend her time, and even who to marry. This lack of autonomy eroded her sense of self-worth; she had no opportunity to trust her instincts or learn from her choices. She told me it wasn't until she got to university – finally in an environment where she could start making her own decisions – that she began to build her confidence. Every small choice, from what classes to take to how she spent her weekends, helped her realise she could rely on herself, and she began to trust her ability to navigate life.

Her story reminded me of an important lesson: **confidence is strengthened through having a sense of agency, making our own decisions and trusting the outcomes, whatever they may be.**

Below are my tips to help you practise trusting your own decisions. Whether it's a big decision, like choosing a house to buy, or something smaller, like deciding between vendors for a work event, the advice below can help you approach decision-making with more clarity and assurance. **Practising assured decision-making – even when you don't necessarily feel confident – helps you cultivate self-trust that will build over time.**

Define your desired outcomes

Before you can make a decision, you need to work out what exactly you're hoping to achieve by making this decision. If you're moving jobs, are you looking for better career progression or more money? If you're deciding where you want to move house, are you looking for more space or an easier commute to work? If it's a mixture of a few things, work out which you want to prioritise and which you can compromise on.

Defining your desired outcomes gives you a clear sense of direction, which makes decision-making feel much less daunting. When you know exactly what you're aiming for, it's easier to trust yourself and feel confident about your choices. Remember, it's about what *you* want, not what others expect of you or what you think you 'should' want.

Compare and contrast
In a notebook or journal, write a list of pros and cons for each option you're deciding between. Seeing all the important information written down in front of you can help you weigh up the costs and benefits in your mind and provide mental clarity, making you feel more in control of your decisions.

Listen to your gut
We all have a little voice inside us that *knows* the right decision, before we even write the pros and cons list. The trick is to tune in and listen. Before you make the final call, imagine that the decision has already been made: close your eyes and imagine each potential future in turn. Notice your emotional and physical reactions. Does one option fill you with excitement or calmness, while the other feels heavy or unsettling? Trust these signals: **gut instinct is a real thing**.

Commit
Once you make your decision, take a leap of faith and throw yourself into it wholeheartedly, rather than constantly looking back and thinking, 'What if I did things differently?'

Remember that there's no such thing as 'good' and 'bad' choices – no path is perfect, and you will likely experience both joy and setbacks on whichever one you choose. Channel the growth mindset we explored in Step 6: Do Hard Things (page 165) to remind yourself that every outcome is a learning opportunity and avoid regret by remembering that you did the best you could with the information you had.

TRUST YOURSELF AND TRUST THE PROCESS.

Every decision you make takes you one step closer to where you're meant to be.

DO IT YOURSELF

We've already discussed the importance of friendships, connections and community. Humans need each other, and that's something to celebrate. However, there are times when we may rely on others a bit too much, which can lead us to believe we're incapable of handling certain things on our own.

For instance, one of my best friends always asks me to cancel reservations at restaurants for her because she gets too nervous to make the call herself. For years, I did the same thing with my sister, asking her to make difficult phone calls to my parents for me because I wanted to avoid the discomfort. Perhaps you've done something similar – maybe you always rely on your roommate to contact the landlord about maintenance issues because you'd rather sidestep the awkward conversation. Or perhaps you ask a friend to review your social media posts before hitting 'share', feeling more confident with their approval first.

In every relationship, it's natural to fall into habits where we take on specific roles or let others do things for us. And, to an extent, that's perfectly fine. I'm not saying you shouldn't rely on people, accept help or delegate tasks when needed. What I *am* saying is that there's power in proving to yourself that you can handle something on your own.

As a boss, one thing I've noticed is that to build confidence in my team and help them grow, I have to make sure I don't fall into the trap of micromanaging them. This is because I know that their competence, and confidence, will only grow if I give them the space to make their own decisions and solve problems independently.

> **Try this:** Every so often, challenge yourself to handle something on your own, even if it feels uncomfortable at first. Here are a few ideas:
>
> - Attend a social event solo instead of asking a friend to come for support.
> - Make a dinner reservation yourself instead of letting someone else take the lead.
> - Send an email to your boss without asking a colleague to review it first.
> - Negotiate prices or discuss finances yourself, rather than leaning on a friend to handle it.

USE VISUALISATION

Often, we feel nervous about situations simply because we don't know what to expect. This reaction is completely natural – our subconscious minds are wired to resist uncertainty, and our brains feel most at ease with what is familiar.

In an interview for *RISE with Roxie*, Dr Tara Swart shared a simple yet powerful strategy she uses to calm her nerves before speaking events. Whenever she's scheduled to give a talk, she asks the organisers for a photo of the room beforehand. This allows her to visualise the event in advance, clearly picturing herself stepping onto the stage and delivering her speech with confidence. By doing this, Tara's brain becomes familiar with the setting, reducing the production of cortisol – the stress hormone – and helping her feel calmer and more assured when the moment arrives.

I love this approach, and it's something we can all use to step into the role of our best selves. Visualisation allows us to mentally rehearse situations so that when we encounter them in real life, they feel familiar rather than intimidating.

▶ EXERCISE: VISUALISE SUCCESS

When preparing for an upcoming situation, whether it's a presentation, a job interview or a social event, use this simple visualisation. Find a quiet space and get comfortable:

1. **Get into position:**
    - Lie down with your arms by your sides, palms facing upwards, allowing your body to fully relax.
    - Alternatively, sit comfortably in a chair with your feet flat on the floor, or cross-legged on the ground. Keep your spine straight, and feel the crown of your head lifting towards the sky.
2. **Visualise the event:**
    - Close your eyes and use your imagination to visualise the future event in as much detail as possible. Picture the colours, sights, sounds and even smells of the environment.
3. **Step into your most confident self:**
    - Imagine yourself entering the scenario as your most confident self. Picture how you walk into the room, how you feel and how you carry yourself. See yourself speaking or interacting with ease, radiating assurance through your body language, facial expressions and energy.
4. **Focus on success:**
    - Instead of imagining worst-case scenarios, focus on everything going well. Visualise people responding positively to you, see yourself achieving your goal and immerse yourself in the feelings of joy, pride and fulfilment.

Visualisation helps your brain feel familiar with a situation before it happens, making it less intimidating. By mentally rehearsing success, you create neural pathways that make confidence your default when the moment arrives. This practice doesn't just reduce stress – it empowers you to step into your best self, ready to face anything.

Next time you're preparing for a big moment, take a few minutes to visualise success. You might be surprised by how much calmer, more focused and confident you feel when the time comes.

DRESS THE PART

A significant part of my confidence journey has been about embracing all the different facets of who I am (or, as I referred to earlier, 'embracing the slash' – see page 155). Rather than limiting myself to a single identity, I celebrate every side of me: a mother, a speaker, a coach, a romantic partner, a feminine woman, a wellness enthusiast, a homebody who loves nothing more than being cosy, a confidante and, sometimes, someone who just wants to dance to wedding music. Depending on the occasion, I choose to express a different aspect of myself, and how I dress plays a key role in that expression.

Dressing in a way that reflects your best self can help you embody confidence more fully. This isn't about impressing others or keeping up with trends; it's about dressing in a way that makes you feel empowered, authentic and comfortable in your own skin. Your clothing choices can act as a kind of armour, helping you feel ready to take on challenges, command a room or engage in meaningful interactions. When you choose your outfit intentionally, you might notice that you stand a little taller, walk with more purpose and project an air of confidence. Dressing intentionally also communicates to others who you are and how you want to be perceived.

When I made the decision to show up as my most confident self, one of the first steps I took was a massive wardrobe clear-out. For each item of clothing, I asked myself, 'Would my most empowered self wear this?' If the answer was no, it was gone. This process wasn't just about decluttering – it was a powerful way of aligning my outward appearance with the vision of who I wanted to become. It's an exercise I highly recommend trying for yourself.

> **Try this:** Next time you have a big meeting, presentation or event, choose an outfit that represents how your most confident self would dress. Think about what makes you feel powerful and comfortable – whether that's a well-tailored blazer, a bold colour or a piece of jewellery that holds meaning for you. As you go through your day, notice how your choice affects your mood, posture and interactions. Dressing intentionally isn't just about how you look, it's about stepping into the energy of your best self and showing the world exactly who you are.

GET COMFORTABLE SETTING BOUNDARIES

A crucial part of stepping into your future self is learning to **set boundaries that protect your time, energy and values**. Boundaries are about defining what is acceptable to you and asserting your needs without apology. When you practise setting healthy boundaries, you show yourself the self-respect you deserve and make space for what truly matters in your life.

The most confident people I know are always the best at this. They don't feel the need to please everyone, nor do they apologise for having limits. They understand that, in order to show up as their best selves, they need to protect their own well-being first. This might mean saying no to extra work, declining social invitations that drain them or carving out time each day for their own self-care. **These confident individuals recognise that their worth is not tied to how much they give to others, but in how they honour their own needs while still contributing meaningfully to the world.**

I know that setting boundaries doesn't always come naturally, especially if you've been conditioned to put others first or avoid conflict. You may feel a pang of guilt or worry that others will see you as selfish. But remember, boundaries aren't about building walls to shut people out – they're about creating healthy guidelines so that your relationships and commitments can thrive.

Boundaries can be powerful confidence builders because they reinforce the belief that you are worthy of respect, worthy of protection and worthy of feeling your best.

> EVERY TIME YOU SAY NO TO SOMETHING THAT DOESN'T SERVE YOU, YOU'RE SAYING YES TO SOMETHING THAT DOES.

Whether it's more time for rest, pursuing your passions or being present with loved ones, boundaries help you reclaim your life in a way that feels true to who you are.

When I started practising setting boundaries, I realised that I had so much more space to invest in the people and projects that really mattered to me. Instead of being spread too thin, feeling resentful and always on the edge of burnout, I began feeling more energised and in control of my life. It was transformative to see that saying no didn't make me a bad person – it simply made me a stronger, more confident version of myself.

Below are some practical ways to support you when setting boundaries:

Get clear on your priorities
In order to set effective boundaries, you need to understand what truly matters to you – what are your goals and your priorities? Allow them to help you recognise where you need to put boundaries in place.

Practise saying 'no' without over-explaining
Many of us feel the need to justify our decisions when we say no, often over-explaining to soften the blow or avoid disappointing others. However, a simple, direct 'no' can be just as effective, without all the extra justification. For example, if someone asks for your help but you're already overwhelmed, simply saying, 'I wish I could, but I'm just unable to take on anything extra right now,' is enough.

Be consistent
Once you start setting boundaries, you may face pushback from those who were used to you always saying yes. This is normal – people don't always like change, especially when it impacts what they get from you. It's important to be consistent with your boundaries even when it's uncomfortable. Over time, others will come to respect them, and you'll start to feel more confident in your ability to stand up for yourself.

Use 'I' statements
Once again, 'I' statements really come into their own here. When setting boundaries, focus on how you feel and what you need, rather than blaming others. For example, instead of saying, 'You're always asking too much of me,' try saying, 'I feel overwhelmed when I take on too much, so I need to limit my availability.' This shifts the focus to your needs rather than placing blame, which can make it easier for others to understand where you're coming from.

Start small

If the idea of setting boundaries feels overwhelming, start with small steps. Practise in low-stakes situations – like telling a friend you're unable to meet for coffee because you need some alone time. The more you do it, the easier it will become.

➤ EXERCISE: GET COMFORTABLE SETTING BOUNDARIES

Identify one area in your life where you often feel overwhelmed or drained because you haven't set boundaries. Imagine how your future, confident self would handle that situation. Would they say 'no' to a request that stretches them too thin? Would they communicate their limits clearly to a friend or colleague? Start small and practise expressing your boundaries in a kind but firm way.

FINAL WORDS

The best part about the saying, 'Fake it until you become it,' is that, eventually, you won't need to fake it anymore. You truly will feel as confident as you deserve to feel.

Over time, every small action, every decision to show up and every step into discomfort builds into something extraordinary. The confidence you once had to consciously work on will become second nature – an inseparable part of who you are.

But here's the truth: confidence has always been within you. When we're born, we don't question whether we're good enough – we exist unapologetically, expressing ourselves freely and moving through the world with curiosity and boldness. But as we grow, life teaches us to doubt ourselves. We start to believe the voices and experiences that tell us we're not enough and, over time, those messages bury the confidence we once had.

The truth is, you don't need to create confidence – it's still there, waiting to be rediscovered. This journey isn't about becoming someone new; it's about unlearning the self-doubt, peeling back the layers of insecurity and reclaiming the confidence that has been yours all along.

EPILOGUE

When I think about my own journey, from rock bottom in 2018 to where I am today, the thing I am most grateful for is my reignited confidence. It has been the foundation for every meaningful moment and achievement in my life. Confidence has given me the courage to pursue my dreams, even when they felt out of reach. It has empowered me to stand up for myself in difficult situations – whether it was negotiating career opportunities, advocating for myself in challenging conversations or setting boundaries in my personal life.

And confidence isn't just about the big things, it's in the small, everyday moments that shape how we live and see ourselves. It's the times I walk into a yoga class, undoubtedly the least graceful and least flexible in the room, and don't care how I look because I'm focused on how it makes me feel. It's the moment I approach someone I admire, get brushed off with a dismissive remark and don't let it rattle me – because I know their reaction says more about them than it does about me. It's speaking up in a meeting, even when I'm unsure how my ideas will be received, trusting that my voice matters.

Confidence doesn't mean I never feel scared or doubt myself – it means I trust that I can handle whatever comes my way. It's the quiet reassurance that says, 'You've got this,' even in uncertain times. It's what allows me to embrace the imperfect, the uncomfortable and the unfamiliar without letting fear hold me back.

Whether it's stepping onto a stage, facing a rejection or setback, or making a decision that aligns with my values, confidence has become my anchor. It's what allows me to live life on my own terms.

Living confidently is unbelievably freeing. It's the quiet reminder that you don't need to be perfect or have it all figured out. It's the unwavering belief that you are enough just as you are – and that you are capable of navigating whatever life throws your way.

I want you to experience that same sense of confidence. The kind that helps you navigate the highs and lows of life with greater ease and resilience. The kind that makes you feel capable, worthy and ready to take on whatever comes next. Because when you believe in yourself, you open the door to endless possibilities. Life becomes something you don't just endure but something you actively create.

This journey – your journey – is about remembering who you've always been. It's about reclaiming your birthright to believe in yourself.

Before I leave you on your confident way, let's quickly recap the steps in this book:

In **Step 1: Master Your Thoughts**, we saw how our thoughts shape our beliefs and our beliefs shape our reality. We learned how to disrupt our negative thought patterns by replacing our inner heckler with an inner cheerleader. We explored cognitive distortions and uncovered how we can create a more reassuring internal dialogue for ourselves.

In **Step 2: Act with Intention**, we learned about the power of self-discipline to give us a greater sense of control over our lives. We looked at the benefits of positive habits and routines, and how they can counteract the limiting beliefs we place on ourselves.

In **Step 3: Stop Trying to Be Liked by Everybody**, we acknowledged our innate desire to be liked, while exploring different ways to reduce the hold this has on us. We learned to reduce our reliance on external validation, and we began to understand that what other people think of us has no bearing on who we are and what we're worth.

In **Step 4: Break Free from Comparison**, we learned that comparison is the thief of confidence. We explored helpful ways to overcome our tendency to compare ourselves to others: by reminding ourselves how far we've come, turning envy into inspiration, building a healthier relationship with social media and practising gratitude.

In **Step 5: Celebrate Yourself**, we began to nurture our sense of self-acceptance, so that it can eventually grow into self-love. We learned to overcome shame by respecting and taking pride in our strengths, talents and abilities, while also embracing and accepting all our nuances and differences.

In **Step 6: Do Hard Things**, we looked at how to cultivate a growth mindset. We learned that, when we challenge ourselves, we build our self-belief. We learned that succeeding in something difficult builds our feelings of competency, but that failure is also an essential piece of the puzzle. We explored how to get comfortable with discomfort and use setbacks as an opportunity for growth and expansion.

In **Step 7: Be of Service to Others**, we learned that being of service to others builds our sense of purpose and encourages us to see our value and all that we can offer the world.

And finally, in **Step 8: Show Up as Your Best Self**, we learned that we can step into our most confident selves *right now*. We can fake it until we become it. Even when self-doubt lingers, we can still show up in the world as our best selves. We can use our body language, effective communication, the way that we dress and the boundaries we set to help us do this, until eventually we really do become the very best version of ourselves.

If you have made it this far, I want you to know I am so proud of you and so excited for you, too.

I can't wait to see what you do with your new-found confidence. You might have finished this book, but your journey is only just beginning.

> TRUE CONFIDENCE IS KNOWING THAT YOUR WORTH WAS NEVER UP FOR DISCUSSION: YOU ARE, AND ALWAYS HAVE BEEN, *ENOUGH*.

GLOSSARY

Self-acceptance: When we possess this, we acknowledge and embrace every aspect of ourselves – including our flaws, weaknesses and mistakes. It's not about being a perfect person, or even believing that we are amazing; it's about acknowledging the nuances we all have as human beings and believing that we are worthy of love and acceptance without any conditions or need for improvement.

Self-belief: This refers specifically to our confidence in our own abilities and our capacity to achieve our goals. In psychology, this is also often referred to as 'self-efficacy'. It's about having faith and trust in ourselves, our competencies and our capability to handle life's challenges.

Self-doubt: When we lack confidence in who we are, we become riddled with feelings of fear, uncertainty and hesitation that can hinder us from performing tasks, making decisions or achieving goals. This leads us to second-guess our actions, or even who we are, leading to low self-esteem and low self-worth.

Self-esteem: This refers to the overall judgement and evaluation we make of ourselves – based on our abilities, achievements and how we feel we compare to others. It's about how much value we place on ourselves; someone with high self-esteem believes they have value and are worthy, whereas someone with low self-esteem believes they are worthless. Self-esteem can change depending on successes, failures and feedback.

Self-love: Think of self-acceptance as the stepping stone before self-love. When we achieve self-love, we don't just accept who we are, we prioritise ourselves and treat ourselves with care and respect.

Self-worth: This is the innate belief that we are worth something as human beings, regardless of whether we have succeeded, failed or what others think of us. While self-esteem is conditional on circumstance, self-worth is unconditional.

ACKNOWLEDGEMENTS

To Wolfe, for being my greatest love and joy.

To Noona & Rana, I'm so lucky to have sisters for best friends.

To Mum & Omar, for teaching me the power of kindness.

To Wade, for your constant love and support.

To Claudia, Jen, Diana & Isabel, for being a dream team.

To Arielle, for our mega (and always sunny) brainstorming sessions.

To Lauren & Becca, for believing in me and this book from day one.

SOURCES

Introduction

1 Silverstone, P. H. and Salsali, M., 2003. Low self-esteem and psychiatric patients: Part I – The relationship between low self-esteem and psychiatric diagnosis. *Annals of General Hospital Psychiatry*, 2(1), p. 2; Henriksen, I. O., Ranøyen, I., Indredavik, M. S. and Stenseng, F., 2017. The role of self-esteem in the development of psychiatric problems: A three-year prospective study in a clinical sample of adolescents. *Child and Adolescent Psychiatry and Mental Health*, 11, p. 68.
2 Vogels, E. A. and Gelles-Watnick, R., 24 Apr. 2023. Teens and social media: Key findings from Pew Research Center surveys. Pew Research Center. Retrieved from https://www.pewresearch.org/short-reads/2023/04/24/teens-and-social-media-key-findings-from-pew-research-center-surveys/.
3 Minnikin, M., 29 Feb. 2024. 75% of women experience imposter syndrome in their career. LinkedIn. Retrieved from https://www.linkedin.com/pulse/75-women-experience-imposter-syndrome-careers-michelle-minnikin-5gvve/.
4 Moss, R., 21 Jun. 2016. Women's body confidence is a 'critical issue' worldwide, warns Dove's largest ever report. The Huffington Post. Retrieved from https://www.huffingtonpost.co.uk/entry/dove-global-body-image-report_uk_5762a6a1e4b0681487dcc470.
5 Maslow, A. H., 1943. A theory of human motivation. Classics in the History of Psychology. Retrieved from https://psychclassics.yorku.ca/Maslow/motivation.htm; Wikipedia, 19 Aug. 2024. Motivation and personality. Retrieved from https://en.wikipedia.org/wiki/Motivation_and_Personality.
6 Tong, E., 4 Mar. 2021. Higher income predicts feelings such as pride and confidence. American Psychological Association. Retrieved from https://www.apa.org/news/press/releases/2021/03/higher-income-pride-confidence.

7 Judge, T. A. and Bono, J. E., 2001. Relationship of core self-evaluations traits – self-esteem, generalized self-efficacy, locus of control, and emotional stability – with job satisfaction and job performance: A meta-analysis. *Journal of Applied Psychology*, *86*(1), pp. 80–92.

8 Henriksen, I. O., Ranøyen, I., Indredavik, M. S. and Stenseng, F., 2017. The role of self-esteem in the development of psychiatric problems: A three-year prospective study in a clinical sample of adolescents. *Child and Adolescent Psychiatry and Mental Health*, *11*, pp. 1–9.

9 Liu, Q., Jiang, M., Li, S. and Yang, Y., 2021. Social support, resilience, and self-esteem protect against common mental health problems in early adolescence: A nonrecursive analysis from a two-year longitudinal study. *Medicine*, *100*(4), p. e24334.

10 Lewandowski Jr, G. W., Aron, A. and Gee, J., 2007. Personality goes a long way: The malleability of opposite-sex physical attractiveness. *Personal Relationships*, *14*(4), pp. 571–85; Murphy, S., 16 Sep. 2015. The attractiveness of confidence. Society for Personality and Social Psychology. Retrieved from https://spsp.org/news-center/character-context-blog/attractiveness-confidence#:~:text=To%20get%20an%20idea%20of,a%20boost%20to%20romantic%20desirability.

11 Orth, U., Robins, R.W., 2022. Is High Self-Esteem Beneficial? *Am Psychol.*, 7777(1):5–17.

12 Murray, S. L., Holmes, J. G. and Griffin, D. W., 2000. Self-esteem and the quest for felt security: How perceived regard regulates attachment processes. *Journal of Personality and Social Psychology*, *78*(3), p. 478; Feeney, B. C. and Collins, N. L., 2015. Thriving through relationships. *Current Opinion in Psychology*, *1*, pp. 22–8.

13 Tierney, P. and Farmer, S. M., 2002. Creative self-efficacy: Its potential antecedents and relationship to creative performance. *Academy of Management Journal*, *45*(6), pp. 1137–48.

14 Mueller, J. S. and Kamdar, D., 2011. Why seeking help from teammates is a blessing and a curse: A theory of help seeking and individual creativity in team contexts. *Journal of Applied Psychology*, *96*(2), pp. 263–76.

15 CBC Radio, 25 Nov. 2022. Are we mislabeling our trauma? Why Dr Gabor Maté believes we need to change the way we think about pain. Retrieved from https://www.cbc.ca/radio/

thenextchapter/are-we-mislabeling-our-trauma-why-dr-gabor-mat%C3%A9-believes-we-need-to-change-the-way-we-think-about-pain-1.6661540.

Step 1: Master Your Thoughts

1. Peer, M., 18 Nov. 2024. Instagram. Retrieved from https://www.instagram.com/marisapeertherapy/reel/DCghgjkvgsX/.
2. Dimopoulos, A., 2020. Applicant's self confidence influence in employment interview process according to recruiters perceptions. An exploratory study in Greece. *International Journal of Human Resource Studies*, *10*(2), p. 82.
3. Heim, S. and Keil, A., 2017. Too much information, too little time: How the brain separates important from unimportant things in our fast-paced media world. *Frontiers for Young Minds*, *5*(23).
4. Cascio, C. N., O'Donnell, M. B., Tinney, F. J., Lieberman, M. D., Taylor, S. E., Strecher, V. J. and Falk, E. B., 2015. Self-affirmation activates brain systems associated with self-related processing and reward and is reinforced by future orientation. *Social Cognitive and Affective Neuroscience*, *11*(4), pp. 621–9.
5. Sherman, D. K., Bunyan, D. P., Creswell, J. D. and Jaremka, L. M., 2009. Psychological vulnerability and stress: The effects of self-affirmation on sympathetic nervous system responses to naturalistic stressors. *Health Psychology*, *28*(5), pp. 554–62; BBC Teach, Jan. 2023. The value of positive affirmations for mental health and wellbeing. Retrieved from https://www.bbc.co.uk/teach/moodboosters/articles/zfk346f.

Step 2: Act with Intention

1. Saghir, Z., Syeda, J. N., Muhammad, A. S. and Abdalla, T.H.B., 2018. The amygdala, sleep debt, sleep deprivation, and the emotion of anger: A possible connection? *Cureus*, *10*(7), p. e2912; Gordon, A. M., 15 Aug. 2013. Up all night: The effects of sleep loss on mood. *Psychology Today*. Retrieved from https://www.psychologytoday.com/us/blog/between-you-and-me/201308/up-all-night-the-effects-of-sleep-loss-on-mood.
2. Lemola, S., Räikkönen, K., Gomez, V. and Allemand, M., 2013. Optimism and self-esteem are related to sleep. Results from a large

community-based sample. *International Journal of Behavioral Medicine*, *20*(4), pp. 567–71.
3. Scullin, M. K., Krueger, M. L., Ballard, H. K., Pruett, N. and Bliwise, D. L., 2017. The effects of bedtime writing on difficulty falling asleep: A polysomnographic study comparing to-do lists and completed activity lists. *Journal of Experimental Psychology: General*, *147*(1), pp. 139–46.
4. Amabile, T. M. and Kramer, S. J., May 2011. The power of small wins. *Harvard Business Review*. Retrieved from https://hbr.org/2011/05/the-power-of-small-wins.
5. Jayawardene, W. P., Torabi, M. R. and Lohrmann, D. K., 2016. Exercise in young adulthood with simultaneous and future changes in fruit and vegetable intake. *Journal of the American College of Nutrition*, *35*(1), pp. 59–67.

Step 3: Stop Trying to Be Liked by Everybody

1. Murray, M., 1 Feb. 2016. Dare to praise. The Whole U. Retrieved from https://thewholeu.uw.edu/2016/02/01/dare-to-praise/#:~:text=Researchers%20have%20also%20discovered%20that,same%20behavior%20in%20the%20future.
2. Wolpert, S., 31 May 2016. The teenage brain on social media. UCLA Newsroom. Retrieved from https://newsroom.ucla.edu/releases/the-teenage-brain-on-social-media.
3. Maté, G., 2024. *The Myth of Normal*. Vermilion; Science & Nonduality in partnership with The Hive Studios, 2021. *The Wisdom of Trauma* [documentary].
4. Rorschach.org, n.d. Promoting the ethical use of the Rorschach Inkblot Test. Retrieved from https://www.rorschach.org/.

Step 4: Break Free from Comparison

1. Summerville, A. and Roese, N. J., 2008. Dare to compare: Fact-based versus simulation-based comparison in daily life. *Journal of Experimental Social Psychology*, *44*(3), pp. 664–71.
2. Festinger, L., 1954. A theory of social comparison processes. *Human Relations*, *7*, pp. 117–40.
3. Aubry, R., Quiamzade, A. and Meier, L. L., 2024. Depressive symptoms and upward social comparisons during Instagram use: A vicious circle. *Personality and Individual Differences*, *217*, p. 112458.

4 Ahmad, R., Hassan, S., Ghazali, N. N. and Al-Mashadani, A. R. F. S., 2024. The Insta-comparison game: The relationship between social media use, social comparison, and depression. *Procedia Computer Science*, *234*, pp. 1053–60.
5 Vogel, E. A., Rose, J. P., Roberts, L. R. and Eckles, K., 2014. Social comparison, social media, and self-esteem. *Psychology of Popular Media Culture*, *3*(4), pp. 206–22.
6 MacCallum, F. and Widdows, H., 2018. Altered images: Understanding the influence of unrealistic images and beauty aspirations. *Health Care Analysis*, *26*, pp. 235–45.
7 Riehm, K. E., Feder, K. A., Tormohlen, K. N., Crum, R. M., Young, A. S., Green, K. M., Pacek, L. R., La Flair, L. N. and Mojtabai, R., 2019. Associations between time spent using social media and internalizing and externalizing problems among US youth. *JAMA Psychiatry*, *76*(12), pp. 1266–73.
8 Reid, S., 29 Aug. 2024. Gratitude. HelpGuide.org. Retrieved from https://www.helpguide.org/mental-health/wellbeing/gratitude.

Step 5: Celebrate Yourself

1 Dunning, D., 2011. The Dunning–Kruger effect: On being ignorant of one's own ignorance. *Advances in Experimental Social Psychology*, *44*, pp. 247–96.
2 Peterson, C., Seligman, M.E.P., 2004. *Character Strengths and Virtues: A Handbook and Classification*. OUP USA.
3 Kernis, M. H. and Goldman, B. M., 2006. A multicomponent conceptualization of authenticity: Theory and research. *Advances in Experimental Social Psychology*, *38*, pp. 283–357.
4 Klussman, K., Curtin, N., Langer, J. and Nichols, A. L., 2022. The importance of awareness, acceptance, and alignment with the self: A framework for understanding self-connection. *Europe's Journal of Psychology*, *18*(1), pp. 120–31.

Step 6: Do Hard Things

1 Dweck, C., 2007. *Mindset: The New Psychology of Success*. Random House Publishing Group; Dweck, C., 9 Oct. 2014. Developing a growth mindset [video]. YouTube. Retrieved from https://www.youtube.com/watch?v=hiiEeMN7vbQ.

2 Federer, R., 2024. Commencement address. Dartmouth College. Retrieved from https://home.dartmouth.edu/news/2024/06/2024-commencement-address-roger-federer.
3 Pfitzner-Eden, F., 2016. Why do I feel more confident? Bandura's sources predict preservice teachers' latent changes in teacher self-efficacy. *Frontiers in Psychology*, 7, p. 1486; Bandura, A., 1997. *Self-Efficacy: The Exercise of Control* (vol. 604). Freeman.

Step 7: Be of Service to Others

1 Wikipedia, 26 Nov. 2024. Prosocial behavior. Retrieved from https://en.wikipedia.org/wiki/Prosocial_behavior.
2 Dossey, L., 2018. The helper's high. *Explore*, *14*(6), pp. 393–9.
3 Decety, J. and Lamm, C., 2006. Human empathy through the lens of social neuroscience. *The Scientific World Journal*, *6*(1), pp. 1146–63.
4 Weiss-Sidi, M. and Riemer, H., 2023. Help others – be happy? The effect of altruistic behavior on happiness across cultures. *Frontiers in Psychology*, *14*, p. 1156661.
5 Gupta, S. and Kola, N., 2024. Relationship between altruism and self-efficacy among young adults. *International Journal of Indian Psychology*, *12*(2).
6 Van Tongeren, D. R., Green, J. D., Davis, D. E., Hook, J. N. and Hulsey, T. L., 2015. Prosociality enhances meaning in life. *The Journal of Positive Psychology*, *11*(3), pp. 225–36.
7 Li, L., Khan, A. and Rameli, M. R. M., 2023. Assessing the relationship between prosocial behavior and well-being: Basic psychological need as the mediator. *European Journal of Investigation in Health, Psychology and Education*, *13*(10), pp. 2179–91.
8 Office for National Statistics, 16 Jun. 2023. Public opinions and social trends, Great Britain: 1 to 11 June 2023. Retrieved from https://www.ons.gov.uk/peoplepopulationandcommunity/wellbeing/bulletins/publicopinionsandsocialtrendsgreatbritain/1to11june2023#:~:text=around%20a%20quarter%20(26%25),having%20high%20levels%20of%20anxiety.
9 Hawkley, L. C. and Cacioppo, J. T., 2010. Loneliness matters: A theoretical and empirical review of consequences and mechanisms. *Annals of Behavioral Medicine*, *40*(2), pp. 218–27.

10 Alden, L. E. and Trew, J. L., 2013. If it makes you happy: Engaging in kind acts increases positive affect in socially anxious individuals. *Emotion*, *13*(1), p. 64–75.
11 Lyubomirsky, S., Sheldon, K. M. and Schkade, D., 2005. Pursuing happiness: The architecture of sustainable change. *Review of General Psychology*, *9*(2), pp. 111–31.
12 Rhoads, S. A. and Marsh, A. A. (2023). Doing good and feeling good: Relationships between altruism and well-being for altruists, beneficiaries, and observers. In: World Happiness Report 2023 (11th ed.). Sustainable Development Solutions Network, chapter 4. Retrieved from https://worldhappiness.report/ed/2023/doing-good-and-feeling-good-relationships-between-altruism-and-well-being-for-altruists-beneficiaries-and-observers/#fn73.

Step 8: Show Up as Your Best Self

1 Bem, D. J., 1972. Self-perception theory. *Advances in Experimental Social Psychology*, *6*, pp. 1–62.
2 Ghulati, S., n.d. Albert Mehrabian's communications model. Scribd. Retrieved from https://www.scribd.com/document/344335262/Albert-Mehrabian-s-communications-model.
3 Van Edwards, V., 2022. *Cues: Master the Secret Language of Charismatic Communication.* Penguin Business; Van Edwards, V., 2018. *Captivate: The Science of Succeeding with People.* Penguin.
4 Cuddy, A., 2 Nov. 2011. Power poses [video]. YouTube. Retrieved from https://www.youtube.com/watch?v=phcDQoH_LnY.
5 Rosenfeld, L. B., Grant III, C. H. and McCroskey, J. C., 1995. Communication apprehension and self-perceived communication competence of academically gifted students. *Communication Education*, *44*(1), pp. 79–89.
6 Bower, S. A., 1995. *Assertive Advantage: A Guide to Healthy and Positive Communication.* National Press Publications.

NOTES

NOTES

CONFIDENCE

NOTES